SEXLESS

How

Feminism

Is Failing

Women

To my wonderful husband
and our beautiful children,
this book is gratefully dedicated.

TABLE OF CONTENTS

SECTION THREE: MOTHERHOOD

SECTION FOUR: WORKING MOTHERS

SECTION FIVE: MEN

SECTION SIX: THE MORAL LANDSCAPE

INDEX

INTRODUCTION

Promoting the Politics of Unhappiness

Let's get rid of Infirmary Feminism, with its bedlam of bellyachers, anorexics, bulimics, depressives, rape victims, and incest survivors. Feminism has become a catch-all vegetable drawer where bunches of clingy sob sisters can store their moldy neuroses.

--Camille Paglia

What's wrong with feminists?

For many years now, it has been hard not to notice that many women who label themselves feminists rarely project a mood of happiness. Instead, they seem angry and bitter. What is more, this unhappiness is not the momentary discontent that signifies the normal ups and downs of any life. Instead, it seems to be a bone-deep unhappiness. And while they seem to believe their ill-humor is entirely justified, given that the world is not the way they want it to be, I have reached an alternate conclusion: the very ideas they promote are also to blame. In the final analysis, the policies the feminist movement is advancing today are simply not going to make women's lives better—not even for feminists.

I do not believe this has always been true. At one time, the women's movement stood for universally appealing principles, principles that hardly needed argument to recommend them: women should be respected, and their worth and their contributions to society should, in so many ways, be adequately recognized and valued. Women fought for legal recognition in their individual capacities; they fought for the right to be treated equally with men in a number of settings, such as education and employment, where one's sex was clearly irrelevant to capability and performance. Even women who were perfectly happy with their own *status quo*, housewives and mothers who had no particular interest in attending college or in competing in the corporate world, could readily sympathize and agree with the principles that animated that feminist pursuit. In fact, it was the universal appeal of these goals, their inherent *justice*, which was largely responsible for the early success of the feminist movement.

While some feminists might dispute the characterization that women have succeeded, the results, by any objective measure, are actually quite tremendous. For example, according to the U.S. Bureau of the Census, women earned 58% of the bachelor's degrees, 60% of the master's degrees, and nearly 50% of professional degrees, such as in law and medicine, for the 2008-2009 academic year. By 2007, the number of women with a bachelor's degree or a higher level of education was twice the number it was only 20 years before. This is no small accomplishment, only two generations after the Civil Rights Act of 1964 included women as a protected class.

This is not to assert that there are not frontiers still to conquer for women. But the reality is that social attitudes toward the status of women have changed a great deal in the relatively short amount of time that has passed since the days when feminists focused almost exclusively upon equal opportunity for women. These accomplishments are significant, and it is hard to overstate them. But the question must be asked: are the goals of modern feminism still centered around these ideals? Are the issues which animate today's feminist movement issues that similarly advance the interests of all women in the name of justice and respect? I do not believe so.

Modern feminism has departed from the core principles that inspired its beginnings. Today, feminism is less and less concerned with the real and practical problems confronting today's women, and more concerned with a particular ideology. In fact, some of the problems today's women face can reasonably be characterized as problems that have resulted from the feminist movement *not staying its course*. And in a terrible irony, a good number of modern feminism's preoccupations are bizarrely disadvantageous to many women, especially those women who, at one time, would have exemplified the highest aspirations of the original women's movement. And even worse, some of the ideas advocated by prominent feminist groups, such as the National Organization for Women, can be incredibly divisive of women and horribly destructive of critical values that many women profoundly cherish.

This departure, this disconnection between what women truly need and what modern feminists seem to be pre-occupied with fighting for, is what this book is about. It is about that feeling of discomfort many women have about the feminist movement, about the doubts they harbor over whether it is really advancing their best interests. It is about what women of the last two generations have been taught to believe about the importance of establishing their status in society, and whether feminism is living up to the message of promise that it once had.

This book takes a close look at what today's feminist movement professes to stand for, but not just with respect to their well-known stances on high-profile public policy issues. Instead, it reveals how it represents an entire ideology that attempts to impose a particular mind-set not just upon women, but upon society at large. It shows how that mind-set has seeped into our collective conscience, and has influenced how all individuals— men and women alike—look at the world and at themselves. It explores how feminist ideas, translated into public policy, have brought about both subtle and not-so-subtle shifts not just in the law, but in American culture, on fundamental ideas about the social and personal significance and meaning of marriage, motherhood, and morality. It explains what feminist ideology reveals about what the feminists believe are appropriate and desirable roles for women and men.

In questioning and analyzing these issues, it becomes clearer how modern feminism is, in some very significant ways, working against the best interests of women. One can begin to see how, regardless of the fact that feminists say they are representing today's women, the ideas they are disseminating and trying to instill in young men and women are ideas that will not provide women with greater freedom, happiness, or fulfillment, but, in many and significant ways, much less. In addition, the ideas expressed here also highlight, in contrast, more reasonable and optimistic expectations about the roles of women and men based on their own and on society's welfare.

This book is a personal view of feminism and its fallout, and is not intended to be a scholarly treatise or historical analysis. Many sociologists and academics have already made contributions to the field in that regard. At any rate, I am not aiming primarily at dissecting the "whys" of feminism; like most dissection projects, what you find inside may be interesting, but not always appealing or, for that matter, useful. In the end, this book does not focus upon what drives it so much as *where that drive is heading*.

So the focus here is: what is the feminists' game, really? The answers are not particularly mysterious or complicated, but they cannot simply be dismissed as the usual diet of "progressive" politics, although it has become very apparent that that is integral to the feminist agenda. Exposing the real dangers requires some careful thought about what feminism is really saying, and how that gets put into actual practice in the lives of women. And that is what the pages that follow are about: thoughts and analysis of where the feminist road inevitably leads, and why that road is one that most women of intelligence and integrity should not travel. This assessment is based upon my own viewpoint and experiences, as well as the experiences and views of others, and upon my own reading and research with respect to the questions and thoughts I have had about the deeper implications of both the feminist message, and, by contrast, the roles women actually play in our society.

Clearly, it is not enough to simply criticize and leave a vacuum. I also express my conclusions about what responsibilities and roles must naturally fall upon women by virtue of being women, given the factors that shape modern society. This book examines what opportunities exist today for women to carve out fulfilling lives for themselves, and the steps a true woman's movement should be taking to bring those opportunities to full fruition. The conclusions are based upon observations of how most women actually behave, how they attempt to design their lives in order to find contentment, and an analysis of what that signifies. As such, it says, perhaps, some things that have been said before, but not in a manner that has been expressed to my satisfaction. Accordingly, it is offered here as my perspective on the challenges facing women as they contemplate what values they should adopt and promote moving further into the 21st century.

The aim here is largely apolitical. In fact, one of the primary faults of today's feminist movement is its obsession with political action as the cure for what are, at their core, essentially cultural or social trends or failings, and, more to the point, individual complaints. Like most political movements, and particularly leftist movements, today's feminists individually see their own actions as one facet of a universal movement in an effort to shape the world for some future generation. And while there is validity to the notion that sweeping social changes only happen by concerted movement, it is also true that sweeping social changes are of questionable value if those changes necessarily require the complete surrender of individual happiness. One is seriously driven to wonder about the "selfless" motivations that are compelling today's feminists to "sacrifice" their lives in the service of some future generation, particularly when there is no indication that what they are providing to the future generation will make that generation better off. There are ideas for which sacrificing one's self may be worth the cost, but, as this book shall demonstrate, the prevailing ideology of modern feminism is not one of them.

While the political landscape is not my focus, it must be acknowledged that public policy is clearly relevant to the broader health and well-being of a society. However, the aim here is much smaller, but infinitely more important: what ideas are actually serving women well in their own lives? What public policies are actually helping them as a practical matter, and what ideas can help them to be more successful in their personal endeavors? And, in contrast, what are the consequences of following the feminist message through to its logical end—will it produce a world that will provide to men and women alike a culture and a society in which personal fulfillment is easily grasped? Because, ultimately, that is what is at stake: not the well-being of a political idea, but the well-being of actual people. In the end, it is a hopeful book, one that gives women something to fight for, rather than, like the feminist movement, always seeking out only those ideas that should be destroyed or criticized.

Finally, this book focuses on marriage, motherhood, men, and morality, because these are core matters in which a woman's experience and perspective are critical. It is in these areas where it is important to gauge whether and where the feminists have failed women, and to discern what can be done to remedy the situation. Naturally, women hold opinions on every subject under the sun, but where are the perspectives and roles of women, as distinct from men, particularly critical? The only reason for women to make an issue of their sex in any political sense is by recognizing the unique role women play in American society. There is no unique women's role with regard to the issue of poverty, for example, even if women, as a group, may be affected by poverty more than men. But there is a necessarily distinct perspective of women on marriage and motherhood, because women are an essential participant in those relationships, and their stature within these contexts is assuredly distinct from that occupied by men.

As for morals, I address those moral questions that are related to female sexuality—specifically, sexual activity, homosexuality, and abortion—areas in which modern feminist activists have attempted to corner the debate as to what is best for all women as a group. It is essential to address these issues in discussing modern feminism because it is most often these moral questions which define the substance of the conflict between women who consider themselves feminists and those who do not.

Furthermore, it is in the moral realm where the real heart of feminism reveals itself to be less than forthright in its claim that it is working for the benefit of women, and much less than what our daughters should be striving to advance. At the same time, this book does not address these moral issues, or any other issues, by reference to moral stances as absolutes. On the contrary, feminist positions almost invariably reject moral standards as a basis on which to judge conduct. Therefore, it is more useful, for purposes of criticism, to evaluate feminist ideas from the standpoint that the feminists employ: by measuring, simply on humanitarian grounds, whether the ideas they promote are making the lives of women appreciably better.

Slogging through the world of feminism is not exactly a day at the beach, but it is tremendously important if women are to come to terms with the roles they play, and what roles they need to play, in order to succeed in their lives—and not only for women, but for men and women throughout American society. Any "civil rights" movement that does not have as its goal the betterment not of one discrete group, but of all people, should not legitimately lay claim to our allegiance. All women should be concerned about what ideas are being promoted in their name, particularly when those ideas affect them daily. In particular, women need to realize that today's feminism is not interested in them—that is, it is not interested in real women. Instead, it is interested in an idea of women, and that idea has few hallmarks of actual womanhood. It is a sexless being. But women are sexual beings, and sexuality matters. Modern feminism is trying to erase or negate that sexuality, to subsume it to other interests, and that effort is hindering the success and well-being of millions of American women. The pages that follow will explain why this is so.

SECTION ONE: FEMINISM

Chapter One: What, Exactly, *is* "Feminism"?

Whatever each individual woman is facing; only she knows her biggest challenge. However, if we add up the problems that affect the biggest numbers of women, then issues having to do with physical safety and reproduction are still the biggest. Female bodies are still the battleground, whether that means restricting freedom, birth control and safe abortion in order to turn them into factories, or abandoning female infants because females are less valuable for everything other than reproduction. If you add up all the forms of gynocide, from female infanticide and genital mutilation to so-called honor crimes, sex trafficking, and domestic abuse, everything, we lose about 6 million humans every year just because they were born female. That's a holocaust every year. It makes sense that reproductive freedom is still the biggest issue – because the reason females got in this jam in the first place was because the patriarchal state or religion or family wanted to control reproduction—to decide how many

*workers, how many children the nation needs,
and who owned them in systems of legitimacy—
or even outright slavery.*

--Gloria Steinem

What do people mean when they use the term "feminism"? There may be a dictionary definition that can answer that question, but perhaps it is best to start with Gloria Steinem's take. According to her, feminism is to some extent undefined, but, at its root, it focuses on victimhood: the perception that women, as a group, and by virtue of their sex, are targeted by the rest of society (meaning, necessarily: men) as less worthy, or even worthless, and that society (again, meaning: men) value women only for their ability to produce offspring. And while there may be validity to Ms. Steinem's concerns regarding the safety and value of women, particularly in non-Western cultures, her assessment is not entirely satisfactory as an explanation. The following are a few observations from the perspective of a woman who, you may be assured, did not bear her children for the purpose of providing society (meaning: men) additional workers.

Feminism is a term that has come to describe a sort of floating philosophy. It is applied to an activist movement that has evolved significantly over a fairly lengthy span of time. Feminism does not mean the same thing to all women. The common denominator, allegedly, is that it deals with women. But even more, the term describes an idea that purports to represent all women as a discrete social, cultural, legal, and political class.

Those who describe themselves as feminists frequently disagree with other feminists as to what feminism stands for or what it ought to stand for, and who certainly disagree with what *I* may think it is. Sometimes, very strong disagreements arise among women who might seem to be at the same end of the feminist spectrum. For example, University of Michigan law professor Catharine MacKinnon, generally acknowledged as one of the leading lights in the world of feminist legal theory, contends that virtually all pornography is demeaning to women and should not be entitled to First Amendment protection. But a group calling itself Feminists for Free Expression regards pornography as a matter of feminist civil liberty, and contends that "The answer to bad pornography is good pornography, not no pornography." (Whatever that means.) So much for pornography.

But just as former United States Supreme Court Justice Potter Stewart stated about pornography, "I know it when I see it," one could say the same thing about feminism. Although the term may denote a spectrum of views, it is today usually a fairly narrow spectrum, and the views tend to trend in only one direction. I acknowledge this spectrum here, at the outset, only because I suspect that some of the criticisms leveled at feminism in this book will be met by one feminist or another who will claim that my characterization is unfounded or unsupported, with citations to the contrary. On that point, it is fair to say that almost every conceivable position on a vast raft of issues has been taken by one prominent feminist or another, all of which are argued on the basis of its peculiar ideology. Thus, for example, even though Catherine McKinnon and Feminists for Free Expression may disagree on the value of pornography, it does not absolve either from criticism just because one side can claim that the other is not really what "feminists" "believe." Both sides legitimately lay claim to the title of feminist on the basis of certain core issues, and based upon their distinct perspective about women as a discrete group. Moreover, neither Catherine McKinnon, nor Feminists for Free Expression, despite their disagreement, would likely claim that the other is not really "feminist." They would, instead, probably just concede that there is disagreement on the position feminism ought to embody as an ideology.

Consequently, I have tried to be careful and give a nod to where there may be conflicts as to what "feminism" stands for or what "feminists" believe today, but the characterizations portrayed in this book are accurate, at least with respect to a significant portion of those women who claim to represent the face of modern feminism. Having said that, there are surely things I have missed; it is virtually impossible to absorb and acknowledge the vast body of feminist writings. To the extent that criticisms put forth here are in line with positions taken by one feminist group or another, I can only say that the aim of this book is not to tear down feminism as a movement, but to critique its modern excesses and abuses with a view toward bringing its focus back into the mainstream of most women's lives.

To be considered a feminist today, it is not enough to have a healthy respect and regard for women, or to believe that women not only can become, but are, outstanding executives, lawyers, doctors, politicians, chefs, truck-drivers, and dog-catchers. Although the attitude above reflects my own beliefs, most people would not consider me a feminist. That is because my views conflict with three matters that lie at the heart of the modern movement: first, I believe that life-long heterosexual marriage is a personal and social good; second, I believe that women are better equipped than men, temperamentally, to care for young children, and that caring for children is the most critical responsibility of every parent and of society as a whole; and third, I firmly believe that abortion is morally, socially, philosophically, and rationally wrong. Espousing this viewpoint essentially bars me from being considered a "feminist" in the modern mold, no matter how much I respect women or applaud their accomplishments across a broad range of personal and professional pursuits, and seek the advancement of women in those same pursuits.

While modern feminism is fairly uncompromising on the issues of marriage, child-rearing, and abortion, as acknowledged above, there is little benefit in trying to nail down only one "feminist" position on every single issue addressed in this book. In fact, it is not uncommon to come across inherent contradictions within feminist ideology itself. But again, the primary aim here is not to dissect the picayune details of what feminism is supposed to be by those who espouse its values, but instead, to focus on the contrast between, first, the goals of feminism as it was originally conceived; second, modern feminist ambitions for womanhood and the status of women; and third, a more reasoned and rational approach to defining the values that womanhood should be embodying based upon what women are and how women actually live.

For the purpose of discussion, however, it is necessary to begin this book by trying to state, with some degree of specificity, what we are talking about when using the phrase "modern feminism." As alluded to above, documenting these ideas is not as pleasant as a picnic in the park, but it is necessary to plod through it a bit to see just what the movement really professes. Most men and women are generally aware of what feminists claim to stand for on flagship issues like abortion, but the rest of the movement is too often dismissed as a bothersome haze of vexing notions, especially by people who generally oppose it. As a consequence, many people are not necessarily aware of just how far the movement goes, and what little undercurrents of social disruption are being aided and abetted by the armies of women and men who support it. For people who already oppose modern feminism's more public face, the next few chapters on what *else* it stands for may be disheartening, but they lend much-needed context to the case against it.

It is useful to start by focusing on the National Organization for Women (NOW). NOW is not the be-all end-all of the feminist movement (whatever it may think of itself); however, it is probably the most prominent and well-organized of the feminist organizations in the United States, and many Americans correlate NOW to Feminism with a capital "F". Certainly, NOW purports to represent all women's interests in the American political scene across a broad field of social matters, rather than focusing merely on one or two issues. Consequently, NOW represents, if not every feminist's view, what is somewhat freely referred to here as the "mainstream" feminist view.

Many women associate NOW with legitimate concerns to the civil rights of women—equal pay for equal work, for example. However, NOW's priorities today are largely divorced from these types of issues and from "civil rights," as that term is properly understood (that is, the right to equal treatment under the law), although workplace equality is still a part of their comprehensive agenda. And as they have departed from equality within the corporate and legal world as the pivotal battle front of their gender war, there seems to be a growing chasm between NOW's political focal points and the interests of many, if not most, American women. Even those women who were initially drawn to NOW's efforts are likely finding a growing disconnection not only between the agenda NOW advances and their own views, but NOW's policy prescriptions and their own personal interests.

This chasm becomes even wider when feminist ideas are taken in as a whole body of thought. As expanded upon in succeeding chapters, many parents might be appalled if they discovered the sorts of ideas that their daughters were exposed to in Women's Studies courses at expensive universities, since "feminism" now seems to embrace, without reservation, ideas such as the normalization of homosexuality, the abolition of marriage, and the dismissal of traditional parenthood (and, consequently, the traditional idea of "family").

In order, then, to understand precisely what is meant when referring to "feminism" and "feminists" in this book, it is helpful to start with a brief history and outline of NOW, which serves as a good proxy for the growth and expansion of the feminist movement as a whole, in terms of influence as well as reaching out into the wide variety of matters that shape American culture.

Chapter Two: The National Organization for (Disgruntled) Women

> *NOW is one of the few multi-issue progressive organizations in the United States. NOW stands against all oppression, recognizing that racism, sexism and homophobia are interrelated, and that other forms of oppression such as classism and ableism work together with these three to keep power and privilege concentrated in the hands of a few.*
>
> *Government, our judicial system, big business, mainstream media and other institutions treat many groups in our society like second-class citizens. Pitting us against each other is an essential mechanism for maintaining the status quo.*
>
> *--NOW Website*

How did NOW become the repository of American feminism? The answer is actually very straight-forward. As recounted on NOW's website, the catalyst for the creation of NOW was sex discrimination in employment. Although Title VII of the Civil Rights Act of 1964 made such discrimination unlawful, the social mores of the day virtually insured that the provision would be interpreted in a way that was vastly different from how it is interpreted today. Thus, when the Equal Employment Opportunity Commission (EEOC) convened in

1965 to implement the Act, for example, it voted to continue to allow employers to segregate the sexes in job advertising. Thus, a company with an opening for a secretary or a flight attendant could advertise for women only, and a law firm seeking a litigator could advertise for men only. Hardly "equality."

One year later, in June of 1966, at the Third National Conference of Commissions on the Status of Women, a small group of women dismayed with the EEOC's position as well as the conference's tenor, met informally in a hotel room to discuss their dissatisfaction. The idea emerged that an organization should be formed to speak on behalf of women in a manner akin to existing black civil rights groups that had made headway. Betty Friedan, best known as the author of the ground-breaking *The Feminine Mystique*, was at this meeting, and she was to become the first president of NOW. By October, the fledgling organization held an organizing conference, and could boast over 300 charter members—a rather significant achievement, when you consider the era.

Betty Friedan also drafted the first Statement of Purpose for NOW, which makes for very interesting reading in light of NOW's current agenda. The entire 1966 Statement of Purpose can be read on NOW's website, and the tenor of that document, as well as its specific language, stands out sufficiently that it is extremely helpful to quote portions here in order to demonstrate the tremendous shift between NOW's original mission and its current stated goals.

It is highly probable that few American women today would find much to dispute in the original Statement of Purpose, no matter what their political leanings are. Although one might pick a few holes in the document purely from the standpoint of a woman looking back on where these statements have taken us 40 years later, for the most part, the women who founded NOW were dealing with a real problem in need of a real solution. In fact, that is really the theme of the Statement of Purpose: to identify the problem of sex discrimination and how it has detrimental effects on women individually, and on society as a whole: politically, economically, and ethically. Thus, the Statement from its very outset nicely casts the purpose of the organization:

> The purpose of NOW is to take action to bring women into full participation in the mainstream of American society now, exercising all the privileges and responsibilities thereof in truly equal partnership with men.

> We believe the time has come to move beyond the abstract argument, discussion and symposia over the status and special nature of women which has raged in America in recent years; the time has come to confront, with concrete action, the conditions that now prevent women from enjoying the equality of opportunity and freedom of choice which is their right, as individual Americans, and as human beings.

> NOW is dedicated to the proposition that women, first and foremost, are human beings, who, like all other people in our society, must have the chance to develop their fullest human potential. We believe that women can achieve such equality only by accepting to the full the challenges and responsibilities they share with

all other people in our society, as part of the decision-making mainstream of American political, economic and social life.

Not an earth-shattering statement today, by any stretch. While these sentiments were rather revolutionary at the time, the document backs up its asserted purposes by citing to specific problems and specific points of contention.

But to get more to the focus of this book, here are the document's statements regarding the role of women in society:

With a life span lengthened to nearly 75 years, it is no longer either necessary or possible for women to devote the greater part of their lives to child-rearing; yet childbearing and rearing—which continues to be a most important part of most women's lives—still is used to justify barring women from equal professional and economic participation and advance.

Today's technology has reduced most of the productive chores which women once performed in the home and in mass-production industries based upon routine unskilled labor. This same technology has virtually eliminated the quality of muscular strength as a criterion for filling most jobs, while intensifying American industry's need for creative intelligence. In view of this new industrial revolution created by automation in the mid-twentieth century, women can and

must participate in old and new fields of society
in full equality—or become permanent outsiders.

Given modern feminism's preoccupations, this look back presents quite a revelation. In 1966, the founders of NOW flatly acknowledged that childbearing and child-rearing were "a most important part of most women's lives," and professional interests were viewed as supplemental to this interest, not necessarily in competition with it. Moreover, this discussion of the involvement of women in careers outside the home was cast within two relevant contexts: first, the span of a woman's life; and second, the changing nature of industry.

The document continues:

WE BELIEVE that this nation has a capacity at least as great as other nations, to innovate new social institutions which will enable women to enjoy the true equality of opportunity and responsibility in society, without conflict with their responsibilities as mothers and homemakers. In such innovations, America does not lead the Western world, but lags by decades behind many European countries. We do not accept the traditional assumption that a woman has to choose between marriage and motherhood, on the one hand, and serious participation in industry or the professions on the other. We question the present expectation that all normal women will retire from job or profession for 10 or 15 years, to devote their full time to raising children, only to reenter the job market at a relatively minor level. This, in itself, is a deterrent to the aspirations of women, to their acceptance into management or professional training courses, and to the very possibility of equality of opportunity or real choice, for all but a few women. Above all, we reject the assumption that these problems are the unique responsibility of each individual woman, rather than a basic social dilemma which society must solve. True equality of opportunity and freedom of choice for women requires such practical and possible innovations as a nationwide network of child-care centers, which will make it unnecessary for women to retire completely from society until their children are grown and national programs to provide retraining for women who have chosen to care for their children full-time.

In this passage, one sees the budding idea of the modern feminist movement's view of family and children as adjuncts to other, supposedly more meaningful, pursuits. But at the same time, the document is clear that the focus is on the creation of *choice* and *opportunity* for women, which can hardly be attacked on its own. And, in general, the statement lacks that prescriptive, dogmatic tone that most NOW proclamations contain today.

A few paragraphs later:

WE REJECT the current assumptions that a man must carry the sole burden of supporting himself, his wife, and family, and that a woman is automatically entitled to lifelong support by a man upon her marriage, or that marriage, home and family are primarily woman's world and responsibility—hers to dominate—his to support. We believe that a true partnership between the sexes demands a different concept of marriage, an equitable sharing of the responsibilities of home and children and of the economic burdens of their support. We believe that proper recognition should be given to the economic and social value of homemaking and child-care. To these ends, we will seek to open a reexamination of laws and mores governing marriage and divorce, for we believe that the current state of "half-equity" between the sexes discriminates against both men and women, and is the cause of much unnecessary hostility between the sexes.

In 1966, the stated purpose of NOW was not to oppose or reject marriage or family, but to reform it in ways that were intended to improve it. Moreover, in 1966, NOW specifically sought to obtain suitable recognition for the *social value* of homemaking and child-care—not merely *economic value*—and did not belittle such pursuits. NOW also expressly took the position that hostility between the sexes is not only unnecessary, but *bad*.

And finally, the document concludes with this:

WE BELIEVE THAT women will do most to create a new image of women by acting now, and by speaking out in behalf of their own equality, freedom, and human dignity—not in pleas for special privilege, nor in enmity toward men, who are also victims of the current, half-equality between the sexes—but in an active, self-respecting partnership with men. By so doing, women will develop confidence in their own ability to determine actively, in partnership with men, the conditions of their life, their choices, their future and their society.

Strangely enough, while there are still areas of American society in which one might find that the vision of equality encompassed by this document is not quite met, for the most part, the women's movement, prior to its modern-day incarnation, had been well on its way to meeting the goals stated in NOW's 1966 Statement of Purpose after a decade or two in terms of legal rights and social views of the value of women. Would that they had just stuck a fork in the organization, said, "It's done," disbanded, and let it go at that.

But that is not the nature of such organizations. Ironically, one could argue that, today, NOW itself may be one of the chief architects of *preventing* the achievement of its avowed purpose of helping women to "develop confidence in their own ability to determine actively, in partnership with men, the conditions of their life, their choices, their future and their society." For those young women heeding the propaganda of today's movement, feminism is creating something, but it is hardly the hopeful vision of confidence and partnership aimed at in the 1966 Statement.

Today NOW advances a whole host of policies, many of which are unrelated to its original purpose. Not surprisingly, then, NOW's website adds this caveat, in very prominent type on the page that reprints the 1966 Statement of Purpose:

> NOTICE: This is a [*sic*] historic document, which was adopted at NOW's first National Conference in Washington, D.C. on October 29, 1966. The words are those of the 1960s, and do not reflect current language or NOW's current priorities.

This statement is just a little sly. Let's not kid ourselves: the words of today pretty much mean the same thing they did in the 1960's; we are hardly dealing with Shakespearean linguistic conventions. The allusion to language seems merely a politic way of saying: "NOW has jettisoned most of its 1966 Statement of Purpose to the far-flung limits of the universe, but we don't want to sound too disrespectful of our founders." In truth, the 1966 Statement is woefully unsuitable for justifying NOW's existence today; it is far too tame to suit the policy ambitions of the women who are currently driving NOW forward.

Today, NOW's agenda not only reaches issues that go far beyond and outside of the purview of the original statement, it has completely changed its tone. In stark contrast to the open-minded, solution-seeking freshness of the 1966 document, NOW has latched its talons onto specific social prescriptions with a death-grip determination that belies any pretense that its purpose is to provide a forum that allows all women to find a voice for their common concerns. Thus, while the 1966 statement specifically discusses "equality of *opportunity*," 22 years later, the 1998 Declaration of Sentiments states as its goal "We envision a world where women *have equal representation in all decision-making structures of our societies*." One-time aspirations for opportunity are now demanded as absolute entitlements.

The sea change in NOW's priorities from its inception to the present day can be starkly illustrated by looking at the 2008 presidential election, in which Alaska Governor Sarah Palin had been placed on the Republican ticket as the Vice Presidential nominee. In 2006, at the remarkably young age of 42, Palin became the Governor of Alaska at the same time that she was raising a family. She even gave birth to a son, her fifth child, while in office. Sarah Palin was not a child of the privileged political or social classes; she had no political connections. She had a humble working-class background, and achieved her position through hard work and perseverance. If one simply measured her career accomplishments against NOW's 1966 Statement of Purpose, the conclusion would be inescapable that Sarah Palin represented, in many ways, the culmination of NOW's original defining principle: she had succeeded in a traditionally male professional sphere, and exercised tremendous political power and pull. Further, she did all this within the context of a long-standing marriage to a man who obviously was not threatened by her success, and who must have, of necessity, fully shouldered a fair portion of the family's domestic responsibilities. It is hard to imagine a woman who exemplified the progress made by the women's movement as measured by NOW's 1966 Statement of Purpose more publicly than Sarah Palin.

In 2008, however, rather than being held up as an example to young women everywhere of what they could achieve through determination, optimism, hard work, and confidence, she was instead publicly skewered by most feminists. Why? Because she had committed the ultimate modern feminist sin of opposing abortion, among other ideological transgressions. While NOW acknowledged the historic significance of Palin's status, and used her treatment by the press as a tool for attacking sexist insensitivity by the media, NOW was outspoken in its opposition to her nomination, claiming that Sarah Palin "opposes women's rights" and that her nomination was a transparent attempt by the Republican candidate John McCain to get women to vote "against their own self-interest." Clearly, it is NOW's prerogative to favor whomever it chooses, but its position on Sarah Palin demonstrates both how far women have come as well as how far NOW itself has travelled in the four decades since 1966. NOW's perspective has shifted immensely.

Judging by NOW's stance not only on Sarah Palin, but on other successful women who do not agree with its specific policy agenda, it is clear that, today, NOW is not about the advancement of women *per se*, but about the advancement of a very particular raft of policies that they assert are in the best interests of women, regardless of what other women may assert to be in their own best interests, and no matter how many women disagree with them. Thus, NOW cannot claim that it wants *actual* women to succeed in their *personal* ambitions; instead, it wants only *certain kinds* of women (or even men) to succeed in the context of *NOW's* ambitions.

Within NOW today, there is not only no debate, there is no dialog. Rather than seeking to unite women and to find creative ways of resolving problems common to all or even most women, unless a woman signs onto NOW's particular political platform, it has no use for her, and, even more, will use its considerable clout to do what it can to marginalize her. If there is anything that NOW appears to like less than men, it is women who don't support its particular agenda.

So just what does NOW think all women need today? Unlike 1966, there is no defining "Statement of Purpose" as it had at its inception, although, as stated above, it does have a 1998

Declaration of Sentiments. And among other things, that Declaration has the audacity to claim that little has changed for women since the 1920's. It claims:

> Today, we fight the same reactionary forces: the perversion of religion to subjugate women; corporate greed that seeks to exploit women and children as a cheap labor force; and their apologists in public office who seek to do through law what terrorists seek to accomplish through bullets and bombs.

If this is truly NOW's outlook, it is no wonder it believes that the fight for women is, alas, still very much alive.

Today, NOW is not merely interested in securing substantive and definable rights for individuals. Instead, it appears to want to evolve humanity into something it has never been, and, by any rational assessment, never will be, and certainly not through NOW's efforts. Accordingly, NOW's list of goals:

> We envision a world where women's equality and women's empowerment to determine our own destinies is a reality;

> We envision a world where women have equal representation in all decision-making structures of our societies;

> We envision a world where social and economic justice exist, where all people have the food, housing, clothing, health care and education they need;

We envision a world where there is recognition and respect for each person's intrinsic worth as well as the rich diversity of the various groups among us;

We envision a world where non-violence is the established order;

We envision a world where patriarchal culture and male dominance no longer oppress us or our earth;

We envision a world where women and girls are heard, valued and respected.

As shown by this list, NOW's current agenda is unquestionably broader in scope than, by comparison, the ridiculously modest aims they articulated in 1966. Gone are goals that are not merely attainable, but measurable by any objective or universally comprehensible standards. Today, NOW seeks nothing less than the reformation of the entire world, although it is a complete mystery what, exactly, they mean when they state things like "a world where women's equality and women's empowerment to determine our own destinies is a reality," or "a world where non-violence is the established order," or "a world where there is recognition and respect for each person's intrinsic worth as well as the rich diversity of the various groups among us." This kind of ambiguous jargon is precisely the sort that is frequently used to justify virtually any atrocity in the name of "progress." Even more strangely, NOW apparently seeks to accomplish these monumental goals through such mundane mechanisms as, for example, the amendment of immigration regulations. (And, one has to add, it is difficult to conjecture how abortion will advance, let alone achieve, any of these goals.)

But in order to get a real taste for how NOW proposes to engineer these reforms, it is necessary to get down to particulars. What follows here are some of the "current priorities" that NOW advances today. These excerpts are drawn from NOW's 2008 Conference Resolutions. They are stated here not to provide a comprehensive view of NOW, but to illustrate how far it has moved away from any pretense that it represents the mainstream interests of women as a discrete group. Furthermore, NOW's specific policy positions demonstrate their tactic of creating and establishing small wedges of subversion into existing laws and social institutions.

Each year, NOW's annual national conference results in a slate of resolutions. One can traipse back through a history of NOW's recent resolutions (if so inclined) on its website and through its literature. Although NOW contends that all the matters addressed by their conference resolutions are relevant to women, they do not seem to bear any particular relevance to women *as women*; instead, they seem to be matters of general interest, as though NOW's position is to avow, quite unnecessarily, that all of life itself is relevant to women. The organization seems to have included within its purview matters that would fit within any scheme that includes the governance of all of humanity, with no cohesive or defining aim outside of the usual lengthy "to-do" list of the leftist flank. At a guess, it probably reflects, more or less, simply the pet causes *du jour* of NOW's more radical membership.

The policy issues addressed in the following resolutions rest on the notion that women bear a unique burden on these matters, but no explanation is provided as to why women, by virtue of their sex, should have any particular wisdom or perspective to offer on the points of contention. Thus, while these resolutions are preceded by numerous justifications, when reading the resolutions themselves, it is beyond debate that NOW's resolutions cannot be dressed up as anything other than garden variety leftist fare.

Thus, regarding healthcare problems faced by women and their children, NOW concludes:

> ***BE IT FINALLY RESOLVED,*** *that NOW call for universal single-payer healthcare to be financed by a drastic cut in the Pentagon's bloated share of the national budget.*

Again, let's be clear: there is no problem with NOW wanting to bring attention to unique healthcare problems that are faced by women and their children, particularly if those problems are not receiving the attention that ought to be warranted by their degree of seriousness or pervasiveness. But what is bothersome is that the emphasis is not on addressing the sources or causes of the problems identified or why women should agree on this issue, but only on demanding a prescriptive big-government program that is not only hopelessly inadequate to remedy the problems catalogued, it does not even remotely address the real crux of the issue. In particular, the overriding emphasis on a non-existent fiscal relationship between national defense and healthcare is laughably transparent leftism, and hardly something with which NOW should expect every woman to agree.

NOW also passed a resolution regarding the enforcement of illegal immigration laws:

> ***BE IT FINALLY RESOLVED,*** *that NOW oppose all pending and future requests by local, county and state police to enter 287(g) agreements with ICE* [Immigration and Customs Enforcement]; *that NOW work at the chapter, state, and national levels to eliminate section 287(g)* [essentially, regulations that allow local law enforcement to act as federal agents in enforcing federal immigration laws] *altogether from the Immigration & Nationality Act; and advocate local and state policies limiting the power of police to inquire into the immigration status of victims and witnesses of crime.*

This is a women's issue? This is how women will earn equality, justice, and empowerment? Of course, the laundry list of justifications for this resolution focuses on the (alleged) impacts of this regulation upon women who are illegal immigrants. But even so, what does local law enforcement of federal immigration laws have to do with those alleged impacts as a general matter? Why not craft a resolution that addresses those impacts, rather than shield all illegal immigrants? In reading these resolutions, it becomes clear that they do not concern themselves with women *per se.* Rather, NOW members, intent on government reform, simply crab together some nexus to women, however remote, that justifies gutting some law or another they don't like.

To continue: significantly, NOW (and, it must be stated, nearly every person who proudly wears the badge of feminism) has, for many years, unequivocally tied itself to the advancement of homosexuality and the "rights" of homosexuals. But the focus is *not* on helping to free homosexuals from adverse discrimination, but rather on obtaining legal entitlements for homosexuals, and in particular on granting to homosexual couples a so-called "right" to marry that has been reserved exclusively to married heterosexual couples for centuries:

> **THEREFORE BE IT RESOLVED,** *that the National Organization for Women (NOW) strongly oppose the passage of Amendment 2-the so-called Marriage Protection Amendment-in Florida, which will appear on the ballot on November 4, 2008; and*

> **BE IT FURTHER RESOLVED,** *that NOW join more than 200 other organizations representing labor, civic, and religious communities as a member of Florida's SayNo2 campaign to defeat Amendment 2;*

> **BE IT FURTHER RESOLVED,** *that NOW officially oppose passage of Arizona Proposition 102, which will appear on the ballot on November 4, 2008.*

> **BE IT FINALLY RESOLVED,** *that NOW strongly opposes Proposition 8, the measure to repeal equal marriage rights in California that will appear on that state's ballot in November 2008.*

It is impossible to rationally discern why or how women, by virtue of being women, would have any particular interest in the legitimization of homosexuality. NOW casts the relationship between women and homosexuality in the context of giving special recognition to any discrete group of people that could be said to be "victims" of discrimination, but while that may explain feelings of *empathy*, that hardly serves to demonstrate a convergence of *interests* between women and homosexuals. Even more peculiarly, one of the cited justifications for this last resolution is this:

> *the proposed amendment could adversely impact enforcement of domestic violence laws in Florida; in Ohio, as many as 80 domestic violence defendants took their claim that a similar amendment barred the state from pressing charges all the way to the state supreme court;*

Incredibly, that is a quotation from NOW's resolution verbatim. In other words, giving homosexuals the right to marry is necessary in order to allow the individuals within those relationships the right to sue their "spouses" who beat them up. Hardly a robust defense of the right to marry, you might say. Apparently, run-of-the-mill assault and battery charges lack the cachet that domestic violence charges have; thus, it would be discriminatory to relegate homosexual couples to inferior criminal proceedings.

And finally, of course, NOW's flagship issue, and the cornerstone upon which most feminist groups have rested their agenda: abortion. NOW's 2008 resolution reads:

> **THEREFORE BE IT RESOLVED,** *that the NOW conference reaffirms that a woman's right to choose abortion to protect her physical or mental health is a fundamental right that cannot*

legitimately be abridged by any court or other governmental entity; and

BE IT FINALLY RESOLVED, that the NOW conference encourage NOW chapters to educate their members about any attempts to limit the "health exception" to late-term abortion bans.

As discussed later, abortion remains the single most divisive issue in America, and one which is forever destined to divide all women, whatever feminists may think. Abortion is the dividing line on which feminists refuse to accept any argument and, in many ways, the conflict on this one issue is emblematic of the fundamental conflict between women who consider themselves feminists and those who do not. And the message of NOW's resolution could hardly be clearer: women should have an unfettered right to abort their own children for any reason, at any time.

As stated above, the 2008 conference resolutions are not intended to paint a complete picture of NOW, but to expose the flavor of their current agenda and current priorities. A listing of any achievements or goals that relate to NOW's efforts on behalf of women to obtain equal treatment under the law have been omitted on purpose here, although they still exist, albeit to a lesser extent as a portion of NOW's agenda than they did in decades past. And while one can still quibble with a detail here and there even on those points, it is clear that NOW members and other feminists have worked for and achieved important goals in terms of obtaining civil rights for women. In addition, there are other programs of NOW that are fundamentally sound, such as their efforts directed at highlighting and ending violence toward women and the blatant exploitation of women. But as an overall agenda-driven organization, NOW has largely morphed its mission into the more peculiar territory exemplified by the resolutions outlined above.

Even more, it should be pointed out that the feminists' original position on the issue of workplace equality was different in *quality* from NOW's current resolutions. NOW's founding mission was really no more than what has classically been understood about the ends of civil justice: the idea that people similarly situated ought to be treated equally under the law. It is a proposition with which virtually any individual could sympathize. But that is not the case with most of the other issues that have been adopted under the banner of feminism.

These resolutions are recited here to flesh out the canvas that is a portrait of modern feminism. In *The Feminine Mystique*, Betty Friedan's acclaimed manifesto, she talked about the "problem that has no name," her quaint description of the distress and dissatisfaction many women felt by being hemmed in by all the social pressures that validated only one legitimate role for women: that of wife and mother. Betty Friedan was clearly onto something. But now, apparently, the problem has a name, and that name is: the entire world. Feminists want to run the world, and, peculiarly, actually think they understand how.

Chapter Three: Through the Looking Glass, to the Extreme Wing of the Feminist Movement

Sexism is the foundation on which all tyranny is built. Every social form of hierarchy and abuse is modeled on male-over-female domination.

--Andrea Dworkin

The fact is that we live in a profoundly anti-female society, a misogynistic "civilization" in which men collectively victimize women, attacking us as personifications of their own paranoid fears, as The Enemy. Within this society it is men who rape, who sap women's energy, who deny women economic and political power.

--Mary Daly

As much as NOW has charted for itself a controversial course, it actually represents the more moderate face of the feminist movement. NOW is a meek and timid younger sister to the "gynocentric" or "gender" feminists— the ultra man-haters in the feminist pantheon. The gender-feminists are not concerned with equality so much as indoctrinating young women into a "new" woman-obsessed ideology. This ideology denies and deconstructs the validity of virtually every historical human undertaking, and it does so primarily upon the basis that every dominant feature of western civilization (to say nothing of eastern civilizations) has been irretrievably tainted by male-centered perspectives and priorities. For example, Sonia Johnson, in *Wildfire: Igniting the She/Volution*, writes:

> Women were the first owned, the first ruled people in every race and class and nation, the first slaves, the first colonized people, the first occupied countries. Many thousands of years ago men took our bodies as their lands as they felt befitted their naturally superior, god-like selves and our lowly, animalistic natures. Since this takeover, they have made all the laws that governed our lands, and have harvested us—our labor, our children, our sexuality, our emotional, spiritual, and cultural richness, our resources of intelligence, passion, devotion—for their own purposes and aggrandizement. These have been men's most profitable cash crops.

Wow. To get a more comprehensive portrait of what the gender-feminists believe, Christina Hoff Sommers' book *Who Stole Feminism?* provides an account that leaves one slack-jawed. And where does one find this brand of feminism? Primarily at American universities. The feminist movement is not content to wage its battles solely on the political and social fronts; rather, it has wholeheartedly embraced the idea that it will not succeed until it tutors and trains young recruits for the cause. Universities are steeped in feminism's excesses and, what is more, these ideas have spread far beyond the narrow discipline of what is harmlessly, if deceptively, called "Women's Studies."

Equal treatment of men and women under the law is not a goal of gender feminism. It is not even an *interest* of gender feminism. Instead, it seems to regard the rule of law, itself, as a patriarchal concept intended solely to dehumanize and oppress women. (Just for the record: this is not a joke.) The word "patriarchal" itself is the ultimate insult; anything that can be labeled "patriarchal" is automatically and unquestionably considered adverse to the interests of all women everywhere. Any viewpoint or institution that earns the appellation "patriarchal" has received what amounts to a gender-feminist death sentence.

In this peculiar world, being a woman seems to be *exclusively* about being the victim of a patriarchal society. And while being a woman, just by itself, confers victim status, it helps to be further marginalized than that. For example, it helps to be a lesbian, and a minority, and disabled, and a vegan. And then you have to be angry about everything that is male, heterosexual, white, able-bodied, and meaty. Gender feminists operate under the premise that all social conventions and institutions have been designed by men, specifically and exclusively, to render women powerless. And yet, for propounding this unreasonable hypothesis, a gender feminist can get tenure at a leading university, a six figure salary, and every male faculty member and administration official cringing and running for cover whenever she shows up in their offices. This is what it means to be "powerless" in the gender-feminist world.

Another characteristic of gender feminism appears to be its obsession with sex, hence the term "gyno-centric." The extrapolation of nearly any gesture or act into a sexual metaphor is like encountering Freud on steroids: to the gender-feminist, a cigar is never just a cigar. Everything seems to have a sexual connotation, or worse: a violent sexual connotation. If a man puts ketchup on his hot dog at a baseball game, it may be interpreted as a subconscious expression of his innate desire to overpower all women through rape, directly provoked by his witnessing a traditional competitive male pastime that involves bats, balls, and getting around the bases to score.

The amazing thing, though, is that people actually take this nonsense "scholarship" seriously, especially institutions of higher learning. Fifty years ago, women would have been looked at sideways if they had even hinted at sporting such outlandish ideas. Today, they roam the halls of academia and throw their weight around university admissions offices, sports programs, history courses, literature courses, and, probably, the glee club. And in return for stirring up this strife, just what is it that the pseudo-academic discipline of Women's Studies provides to the world of higher learning, to young women, to the workforce, and to society in general? By any objective measure, all it does is encourage young women to view the world through the same distorted, hopeless, joyless, victimized lenses as their feminist professors. Hooray for feminists! Even more, the ability of these radical feminists to send the administrations of their schools into a tizzy over any allegation of sexual insensitivity or "patriarchal" condescension is a testament to the success of this movement. They have made virtually every program these universities operate into an uncharted minefield of potential lawsuits, siren-calls for mandatory awareness "ovulars" ("seminars" is a sexist term), and an assortment of other nagging issues that translate into needless expense and bad publicity.

Gynocentric feminists embrace with relish the irrational nature of this new academic "discipline," since reason itself is masculine or, at least, the elevation of reason over irrationality is a concept imposed on women by a male-dominated culture. Again, this is not a joke; this contention is a hallmark of feminist ideology. Under such a scheme, however, truth necessarily becomes subjective, because when reason is thrown out the door, truth is neither objectively verifiable nor universally applicable. As a consequence, in gender feminist philosophy, virtually every idea is entitled to equal merit, no matter how bizarre. Ideas flourish and proliferate without rigorous analysis or criticism.

Feminist legal theory is a perfect illustration of the gender-feminist's peculiar perspective. While anyone with a weak stomach or a strong sense of . . . well, *sense*, would be well-advised to steer clear of feminist legal theory, it is tremendously revealing of the peculiar gender feminist mindset. If you were to Google "feminist legal theory," a wide variety of sites would pop up, such as a Feminist Law Professors blog and a collection of other sites with indecipherable essays. One of the more eye-opening sites is the one for the *Yale Journal of Law and Feminism*.

Yale Law School is generally considered the top-rated law school in the nation, which suggests that it stands in the vanguard of legal theory and scholarship. On its site, the *Journal* proudly proclaims:

> The *Yale Journal of Law and Feminism* is committed to publishing pieces about women's experiences, especially as they have been structured, affected, controlled, discussed, or ignored by the law. These experiences include the particular experiences of women of color and

> of lesbians. We encourage submissions of
> articles, essays, and reviews on any subject
> bearing upon the intersection of law and
> feminism. We have organized the Journal to
> reflect our feminist values: we make major
> decisions collectively, by modified consensus.
> We encourage one another to speak at meetings
> and strive to ensure that all members feel
> comfortable participating.

Tellingly, while the *Journal* happily professes its fuzzy feelings
about sisterhood, it does not make any claims respecting the value
or legitimacy of its content. It does not profess to be academically
rigorous or relevant to the practice of law. Instead, it is more
interested in fleshing out the contours of identity politics and
touting its collective decision-making credentials. This is,
unfortunately, typical of much so-called feminist "scholarship."

But even more bewildering is the *Journal*'s logo. The
logo depicts three versions of Lady Justice—the traditional figure
of a blindfolded woman holding a scale. For anyone who had
thought the symbolism of Lady Justice was rather straightforward,
the Journal's analysis is a bizarre revelation. The cover of the *Yale
Journal of Law and Feminism* depicts three versions of Lady
Justice, of obviously varying ethnicities, holding their scales, but
lifting their blindfolds: very profound. This is the explanation:

> Justicia—our icon of justice. She sits or stands
> above courthouses or in courtrooms, supposedly
> overseeing and inspiring choices between right
> and wrong. And we trust in her competence—
> until we are confronted with a body of law such
> as sex discrimination law, in which so much

seems unjust. Thus, we approach her. Is she really what she seems?

At first glance, we are reassured—Justice is, after all, a woman. She must understand us. . . . If Justice is a woman, surely this fact should argue for women's *inclusion* in the sphere of law.

But, as we again look at our icon, a troubling reality confronts us: Justice is not simply a woman, she is a *blindfolded* woman. Why this blindfold? The standard assumption among legal scholars is that Justice herself tied it. But if we accept this explantion [*sic*], we must wonder why Justice chooses to separate and distance herself. Does she not consider the circumstances of a dispute relevant to its resolution? . . . . Perhaps Justice is not a feminist.

Or perhaps Justice did not choose to be blindfolded. In such a case—where Justice was blindfolded by someone else—our suspicion that Justice has been "similarly situated" appears verified. Blindfolded, Justice cannot see that she is a woman; not realizing that she is different from other women, she is deprived of all the advantages and disadvantages such recognition would bring.

It may be true, as many have observed that the blindfold ensures Justice's impartiality towards those with more power and influence than she.

But at the same time, the blindfold ensures Justice's impartiality towards those with *less* power than she, those who are, in some sense, disadvantaged. Unable to see whatever systemic disadvantages this latter group faces, unable to see her own membership in such a group and thereby possibly understand the nature of their plight, Justice can make her decisions based only on a limited set of facts before her. . . .

We may hope that Justice, though blindfolded, realizes her gender through non-visual means. From a feminist standpoint, the blindfold may even have served some positive purpose, in heightening Justice's other senses, allowing her to "see" what may not always be visible. But the time has come to fully restore Justice to *all* her senses. It is time Justice employed *all* her powers in overseeing the law. It is time she cast off her blindfold.

Imagine: some poor parents are shelling out over $46,000 a year so that their daughters can learn to think like this. This is the sort of painstaking and frankly asinine deconstructive over-analysis of an issue that is common within the Women's Studies realm. And it is taking over other liberal arts disciplines, as well—history, art, literature—as well as law schools.

At the extreme, the feminist lawyer is not content to help a poverty-stricken, welfare-reliant single mother to get the child-support and alimony her cheating and deserting husband owes her because he's a scoundrel, he violated the law, and he has sufficient assets. For the feminist legal theorist, the law must be altered to incorporate her pet legal theories. Accordingly, an alimony/child support case can be used to condemn the larger social implications of this woman's status as a victim-female and society's complicity in oppressing and subjugating all women. Thus, by forcing this woman to endure the ordeal of enforcing antiquated and male-defined laws that require her ex-husband to be financially responsible for supporting her based upon the mere fact that he once married and impregnated her, the law is actually subjugating this woman further to this man and thereby perpetuating male hegemony with respect to all women. After all, what are clients for, but to give feminists the means to retool society? For the record, I just made up this theory of alimony/child support on-the spot. But, upon reflection, it is a fairly sound example of feminist theorizing—which only goes to show that feminist theory is not particularly intellectually challenging; it is just a bit of contortionism. Feminist theory simply requires grafting onto any scenario the context that all men are oppressors, all of society is patriarchal, and all women are victims.

Feminist legal theory falls under a number of titles, and contrary to popular belief, very little of it rests upon the presumption that all people should be treated equally under the law. In actuality, most of feminist legal theory rests upon the opposite contention: the law should treat people *differently*. For example, in February of 2009, a woman wrote an article for the California Bar Journal in which she argued that the law should also account for *cultural* differences in applying the law. Thus, she pointed out, a Hispanic man should have been treated more leniently when he killed someone for insulting his mother, since that is considered a grave and provocative act in his culture. And an Armenian man denied access to his children for touching his daughter's genitalia should not have been treated as strictly, because it is not taboo to do that in the Armenian culture. Do the people that advance this kind of twaddle even think about what they are saying, about the practical implications of adopting a subjective system of law that treats all people differently based upon whatever values they happen to espouse? Do they care?

But this kind of thinking is a natural product of feminist legal theory, the theory under which Justice is not blind at all, but gets to do whatever she feels like on a given day to satisfy her own ideas about what justice requires. Accordingly, under one branch of feminist legal theory, women are not merely permitted to be irrational, but should *be expected to* behave irrationally; and it is this very irrationality that ought to excuse them from legal culpability or any variety of personal responsibility for their behavior. In essence, the theory goes, the rational woman acts irrationally.

The Anita Hill/Clarence Thomas hearings are a perfect illustration of this theory in practice. It is one reason why Anita Hill, to this day, is a feminist icon. To revisit this debacle: during Senate hearings upon Clarence Thomas being appointed to the Supreme Court, Ms. Hill stepped forward to testify that Mr. Thomas, when he was her boss, treated her to frequent, unwelcome, and distastefully graphic discussions of pornographic movies. Before discussing this further, however, let's establish one fact from the outset: only Anita Hill and Clarence Thomas know what happened between them, and even then, one can't be too sure. But the bottom line is that many people, including, apparently, the members of the Senate Judiciary Committee, had difficulty wrestling with the idea that a bright and capable woman such as Ms. Hill would willingly not merely continue working with a man, but agree to transfer to a new and different job with him at a different employer, if she thought he was . . . well, creepy.

But to feminists universally, this is perfectly acceptable and understandable behavior. And, given some of the strange things women have done, it would not be beyond the realm of possibility. What it is beyond is the realm of common sense and good judgment.

But to this day, that episode seems to mark the day when open and overt war was declared between the feminists and the masculine world. It served as a rallying cry, and a declaration of solidarity: the "I believe Anita Hill" bumper sticker. That cannot have been Ms. Hill's intention. It was hard enough to testify as she did; and, even if she were a feminist (or especially so), one can only imagine how mortifying it must have been to be made into the poster child for feminist victimization. But there it was. The Anita Hill episode was polarizing. And some of it might even have been a good thing, as uncomfortable as it was for everybody to endure it or witness it. It certainly served to "out" the more disgusting examples of masculine office boorishness, as well as highlight the existence of true *quid pro quo* harassment. But it also united the feminist frontline, from the staid NOW vanguard to the academic "rad-fems." For the hard-line gynocentric feminists, the Anita Hill debacle gave them the opportunity to point the finger at men, as though this ridiculous farce served to demonstrate to the world that all men are no better than a bunch of lewd and randy adolescents who use their power primarily and purposefully to belittle women through sexual domination.

Gender feminism does not balk at making such excessive and extravagant claims. Women's Studies "scholarship" advances untried and bizarre theories about the injustices of society, as though these theories can adequately explain, validate, and justify the personal misery of women who wallow in the bitterness that gender-feminism promotes. But these theories seem more the product of intellectual invention than the product of any practical experience or serious and intelligent reflection. And, unfortunately, the only economic use of these skills seems to be to get a job teaching other young women to be similarly discontent.

That is perhaps the most peculiar irony—and gravest failing—of college courses and majors in Women's Studies. It is also the hazard that feminist theory presents when it insinuates itself into more legitimate academic disciplines. Back in the day, some really intelligent women, some of whom were yesteryear's feminists, sought to abolish the traditional and old-thinking academic concentrations of, for example, Home Economics, decrying such a course of study as oppressive, limiting, and derogatory to the women who were channeled into it. But Women's Studies, as a major, seems to be an infinitely more idiotic pursuit than Home Economics. Instead of learning skills which would at least have some practical value such as cooking or sewing, Women's Studies feeds young women a stream of unmarketable intellectual drivel. Yet the primary—and absolutely valid—goal of the *original* feminist movement was to make sure that women were given opportunities to exercise and apply their intellectual gifts in areas that were historically foreclosed to them. Even idle, wealthy young women of the 18th century—who were taught to make lace, draw, play music, and sing—learned skills which, today, could actually provide a woman with a decent or even highly lucrative career. But Women's Studies courses, in stark contrast, actually *deprive* women of the tools and the training they need to obtain economic control over their lives.

Today's young women would be better served both personally and professionally by obtaining hard degrees in subjects like engineering, medicine, architecture, pharmacology, biology, chemistry, geology, or, for that matter, medieval French literature, than in Women's Studies. For all their incessant talk about empowering women, feminists rarely state the uncomplicated truth: young women need to learn and to develop marketable skills. When they do not, they doom themselves to being at an economic disadvantage, no matter what paths their lives take. History demonstrates that economic vulnerability, as a rule, translates into personal and political disadvantage. As noted above, this is the key lesson the earlier feminist movement sought to hammer home to all women and to American society in general. As noted in NOW's 1966 Statement of Purpose, feminist pioneers like Betty Friedan understood that unless women were given the ability to participate fully in the economic marketplace, women would forever be relegated to second-class citizen status.

But, Women's Studies, as an academic discipline, shuts off whole avenues of opportunity. Rather than taking full advantage of the educational opportunities available to them at university—opportunities, by the way, which *the original feminists worked so hard to provide to them* and which would enable them to acquire the economic power that is their best means to achieve control over their futures—young women are, ironically, channeled into frittering away their undergraduate years being told by feminist professors that society has conspired to deprive them of the means to succeed. Women are encouraged to indulge themselves in the status of victimhood. They are not instructed that independent economic well-being and the acquisition of authority and influence are a matter of garnering a useful education, mastering practical skills, cultivating and applying a sound work ethic, and developing strength of character. Instead, they are told that these things can only be achieved for women through a collective effort to advance feminist social and political policies aimed at "social justice." As a result, Women's Studies likely does more to handicap the young women who succumb to its message than any "oppression" the outside world is supposedly heaping upon them. Rather than being told that their goals are achievable whatever obstacles they may encounter, they are instead taught to focus on the obstacles themselves. This is unforgiveable in anything calling itself feminism, particularly when so many tangible examples abound of women who have succeeded rather spectacularly despite our supposedly oppressive culture.

There is, in addition, a more mundane reason that women should be diverted away from Women's Studies courses: other courses of study would at least force young women students to confront the manifest reality that the world does in fact contain men. Women's Studies courses are the exclusive province of women, except for the occasional confused or intellectually curious male. Consequently, women who pursue such courses have fewer occasions to learn to relate to men. Yet, if our society is to have any hope at all, there is an absolute need for women to learn to get along with and forge positive, productive relationships with men.

In virtually every way, gynocentric feminism condemns men, and not just based on the belief that men have been misled or poorly trained through education or culture. To them, men are *inherently* oppressive. Gynocentric feminism is that feminism which, to put it in readily understandable terms, posits all men as *potential* rapists and all women as *actual* victims. Thus, in a characterization typical of feminism, Marilyn French had her heroine in *The Women's Room* assert:

> Whatever they may be in public life, whatever
> their relations with men, in their relations with
> women, all men are rapists and that's all they

are. They rape us with their eyes, their laws, their
codes.

Which leads one to ask: what hope is there, then, for a
constructive and congenial future for men and women? If men
cannot even be *raised* in an acceptable way, then gynocentric
feminism necessarily sees society as doomed. And, in fact, this
does seem to be a fundamental problem for gender feminists. No
matter what happens to them or around them or, for that matter, to
anyone else, they seem to plug it into some magic formula that
translates the event into yet another demonstration that the world is
overwhelmingly oppressive to women.

As extreme as this more radical brand of feminism is, it is
not going away. Instead, it seems to be gaining purchase among a
select group of individuals, which would not be so bothersome but
for two facts: one, those individuals have a great deal of influence
in our society and in our educational institutions; and two, those
individuals have no interest in anyone's well-being or happiness,
least of all their own. In fact, nothing can make these feminists
happy, since the whole point of their discipline seems to be to
invent new ways of looking at the world that infuriate them.

But even stranger is how docilely the rest of society is
accepting of this insanity. This feminism that encourages irrational
anger, animosity, and discord is not only allowed to go unchecked,
it is encouraged to proliferate and to blossom into ever more
outlandish theories about the ways in which men ought to be
ostracized, condemned, and castrated (and, given the vehemence,
this last would be meant both figuratively and literally). And while
radical feminists like to paint our "patriarchal" culture as though it
is run by ham-handed, sweaty brutes hopped up on testosterone,
the reality is that these feminists wield such a nasty punch of

venom that everyone has been cowed into stunned silence while they go traipsing through the academy unmolested. When it comes to Women's Studies, our universities hardly foster an atmosphere of robust intellectual debate and inquiry. Gender feminism, perhaps more than any other academic discipline, is in tremendous need of critique, analysis, and scrutiny, yet little is applied. Women's Studies "scholars" are given free rein to discuss their grandfathers, fathers, brothers, and, if they had them, husbands and sons, as though they are a menace. To be sure, men and women are vastly different; as Jack Lemmon said in *Some Like it Hot*: "I tell you, it's a whole other sex!" But that does not make men and women "natural" enemies, whatever these bitter women may believe. No one should tolerate the idea, without question, that men and women were created basically to beat up on one another.

Finding common ground was what the civil rights movement was about. It is what the original feminist movement started with: treating men and women with equal respect, treating them as equal under the law. In every other social arena, Americans are badgered relentlessly on the supposedly desperate need to embrace "diversity." But apparently, Americans need to respect, understand, appreciate, love, and accept everyone in the world except men. The gender-feminists, virtually alone, are getting a pass from the rest of society. People have been intimidated so thoroughly into appeasing this intolerance one almost expects the federal government to begin hearings to consider doling out gender-reparations to make up for America's shameful history of being governed only by men.

As this constant diet of anger and resentment makes absolutely no one better off, the question arises: what, exactly, is the point of gender-feminism? And even more baffling is: what does this ideology reveal about these feminists' opinion of women? Treating women throughout history, particularly "common" wives and mothers like their grandmothers and great-grandmothers, as though their lives were meaningless and inconsequential demonstrates an alarming lack of respect and a disgraceful lack of humility. Just what do the gender-feminists contend that these women were supposed to have done with their lives? The Women's Studies perspective seems to have adopted the dim-witted proposition that only their kinds of ideas, and their kinds of lives, have any worth or meaning. This perspective manifests itself in the gender-feminists' contempt for most women, and for all men. While contempt and disrespect for others is hardly a viewpoint that should be encouraged in anyone, it is especially unattractive in young women attending university whose experience of the world is already limited.

Rather than opening up the wealth of life's opportunities available to today's young women, Women's Studies puts blinders on them, giving them distorted and bizarre ideas of what their lives' endeavors ought to be. This is not how women should want their daughters to grow up. This negative, bitter outlook on history, on men, and on life is not a healthy feminism.

Chapter Four: The Brave New Feminist World

My goal in life is to change the entire social and economic structure of western civilization, to make it a feminist world.

--Marilyn French

Just what is it that the fully realized woman ought to strive for in the modern feminist world? After all, the measure of feminism can only be made by assessing just what kind of society it will lead to. What does it value? How do people live and relate to one another? And most importantly: will people be better off? Let's ponder that for a minute.

Based upon research of what the feminists stand for and support, the following is a credible version of the ideal scenario for the ultimate feminist life, judging by the policies they promote and the policies, laws, and social norms they oppose:

> When a daughter is born, she will be born only because her mother decides that having a baby will enhance her own lifestyle; otherwise, the baby would have been aborted at the sole discretion of the mother. She will be raised in a sex-neutral household by a single mom, two unmarried lesbian mothers, two married lesbian mothers, two unmarried gay

fathers, two married gay fathers, an unmarried heterosexual couple, a married heterosexual couple, a single father, or any combination of the above. American society will not really care which, and neither will her parent or parents, who may or may not be genetically related to her, since she was conceived by artificial insemination. If she has two parents, the household chores and child-care responsibilities (that is, those not performed by an institution) will be divided between them exactly equally and performed on a rotating basis between them to avoid any possibility of sexual stereotyping.

She will attend a government-funded and -run day-care facility by government-regulated and -licensed day-care providers who are not allowed to show her any affection or express any endearments for fear of that affection being construed as sexual molestation, favoritism, or harassment, and the endearments as expressions of non-neutral stereotyping of girls that will form in females an unseemly desire to obtain approval or to measure their own self-worth through pleasing others.

The little girl will play with sex-neutral toys or, alternatively, she will be required to spend equal time with an assortment of role-playing toys designed to prohibit any sex-stereotyping; thus, for every hour she plays with a doll, baby stroller, tea set, or cookware, she will have to spend an equal amount of time, hour for hour, playing with a dump truck, pirate ship, superhero action figures, and a construction tool belt. She will not, however, be allowed to play with toy swords, guns, or punching bags, as such toys engender and encourage aggressive tendencies; boys, of course, will also be disallowed from engaging in sex-stereotyping forms of play, up to and including squelching every display of their naturally aggressive or competitive spirits. Of course, no child will be allowed to dress up as a cowboy, princess, bride, or Republican, because such figures either represent sexist stereotyping or suggest the glorification of individuals or groups who have a record of oppressing discrete, politically under-represented minority groups.

The young girl's mother, mothers, parents, father, or fathers will work full-time at high-powered jobs, or maybe not-so-high-powered jobs, where they will be guaranteed minimum compensation exactly equal to everyone else, because that is the only way the government and trial lawyers could guarantee pay parity and the elimination of any likelihood that women, minorities, and the disabled were not being unfairly passed up for promotion. But it won't really matter, because roughly 80% of everyone's income will be taken by the government to fund the government-paid-for day-care, education, contraception services and devices, abortions, healthcare, food, and housing that will be utilized by this young girl throughout most of her life.

The young girl's primary and secondary schooling will be at a government-run public school where teachers are trained to (and disciplined if they fail to) call on girls exactly the same number of times as they call on boys in every subject, and respond to both boys and girls with the exact same degree of approval to any given answer, right or wrong. The children will be instructed in a broad selection of studies, not merely standard subjects such as math and English. In fact, the emphasis on English will be reduced to include, without prejudice, instruction in a variety of other languages proportionate to the native cultures reflected in the student body overall. The curriculum will include: sex education; multiculturalism; the history of American imperialistic aggression; and how to combat global warming by policing your household for unrecycled recyclables and excessive energy consumption.

History, English, and Art courses will address exactly equal numbers of men and women historical figures, authors, and artists; thus, she will have a completely befuddled comprehension of the significance of historical events, literary accomplishment, and artistic judgment. For example, a patchwork quilt will be regarded as having precisely the same artistic value as the ceiling of the Sistine Chapel. The scope of study will be so broad that by the end of the day, students will have spent a total of 10 minutes on mathematics, but it won't matter; that's what calculators are for.

Students at these schools will not be graded on their work, as it may lead to the outmoded concept that self-esteem should be based upon actual achievement. Moreover, grading leads to the impression by students that their own performance is measured by comparing it to the performance of other students, and thus, violating the government ban on competition. Students will, however, be regularly surveyed as to how they feel about a particular subject.

Accordingly, students are also not allowed to play in competitive sports such as dodgeball, baseball, basketball, volleyball, track, or any other activity that includes scoring or beating an opponent. For physical education, students are encouraged to play soccer, but only government-sanctioned soccer in which there are no goals on the field and, hence, no scoring or, for that matter, any object to the game. The children will simply run around in circles kicking a ball. But, of course, no student is actually required to engage in any physical activity whatsoever based upon his or her subjective determination of whether such activity is in the interest of his or her overall physical and mental well-being and feelings of self-esteem.

By the time the young girl attends college, she will be fully versed in virtually every sexual practice known to men and women throughout history, as well as fully informed on every method of birth control, including abortion, as well as the symptoms and treatments of sexually transmitted diseases. She will, however, be blithely unaware of the fact that she could avoid the risk of innumerable health concerns as well as un unwanted pregnancies by the simple expedient of refraining from engaging in sexual intercourse with members of the opposite sex. However, it has occurred to her that she might save herself a passel of trouble by simply becoming a lesbian, which is all the same to her.

She cannot, however, write a simple declarative sentence. On the contrary, the degree to which she comprehends or knows anything in the subjects of geography, grammar, economics, logic, mathematics, history, or science is only sufficient to qualify her for elective office.

At college, she will engage in a course of study that has precisely zero value in terms of providing any service that leads to the production of tangible goods that serves a human need which people would readily purchase in a free market. That is: she will major in Women's Studies. The only compensable value of this degree will be within the halls of academia, where her goal will be to further disseminate and expand upon entirely abstract but critically profound and useless philosophical theories and inculcate them into the minds of other women.

By the time this young woman submits her Ph. D. thesis, not a single living individual will be capable of understanding what she is talking about or be able to have a pleasant conversation over a cup of coffee with her, which virtually guarantees that all who meet her will universally pronounce her brilliant. Consequently, she will earn a tenured chair on the faculty of a prestigious university where she will snag for her sponsoring institution innumerable and unbelievably large government grants to study nothing of particular interest to anybody or, conversely, will, after five years of intensive research and travel to exotic locations, provide conclusions that anyone with five functioning senses and a modicum of common sense could have told you if you had bothered to ask. She will eventually obtain a coveted seat on a prestigious government body where she can do further damage by disseminating her ideas more broadly, and will ultimately serve in the cabinet of some Democratic president or become president herself.

During her long and distinguished career, she will not get married, and she may or may not decide to have children, but the decision will be entirely unilateral. Moreover, she will not become pregnant in the usual way, but by the artificial insemination of one of her cryogenically frozen eggs, which she had harvested at the age of 24 so that she would not be hampered by the inconvenience of a "biological clock" ticking away her fertile years. Consequently, she may decide to have children, or not, depending upon how she feels on any given day throughout her entire life. Moreover, even if she does impregnate herself, she may carry that child to term, or not, depending upon how she feels on any given day throughout the duration of her pregnancy. Any children born to her will be raised precisely the way she was, but she'll hardly be cognizant of that child because her work is infinitely more critical to the world than the raising of children who are loved and taught to be good, responsible, loving, and civic-minded individuals by their own parent or parents.

Finally, at her funeral, thousands will attend and blather on *ad nauseum* about what a shining example this woman was to the rest of womanhood for her intrepid endeavors to enlighten the world, and she will be written up in history books.

That's it. That's the ideal life feminism offers. However facetious it may seem, virtually every aspect of this scenario is based on stated feminist policies and feminist ideology. And because feminism shows little tolerance for alternative opinions, alternative interests, or alternative views, this is an apt description of the world they would like to create not just for themselves, but for all men and women.

And it really should go without saying, but being written about in history books is a fairly pathetic ambition. Is that really the sum of what women want out of life?

SECTION TWO: MARRIAGE

Chapter Five: So, What Have You Got Against Marriage, Anyway?

We can't destroy the inequities between men and women until we destroy marriage.

-- Robin Morgan

The original women's movement began with a universally sound idea: that people should be treated equally *insofar as they are equal*. But being treated equally cannot make two different things the same. When you try to apply the equality principle in the wrong context, the idea of "equality" is meaningless. For example, you might chop apples and peaches in exactly the same way to put them your fruit salad, but to say that an apple is "equal" to a peach is to say precisely nothing. Moreover, it is not demeaning to the peach to say it is not an apple, and calling a peach an apple does not make it any more like an apple. Discrimination, at its core, merely means to draw a distinction between two things. And in a marriage, discriminating between a man and a woman is not only allowable, it is essential.

This section of the book begins the discussion of the contrast between the reactionary feminist vision of womanhood, as illustrated in the previous section, versus the roles traditionally served by women, specifically those of wife and, as discussed later, mother. It highlights the conflicts that were bound to develop between these competing views, and shows how many feminists failed to fully recognize, much less address, the problems that have arisen by attempting to impose a post-feminist culture on a society predisposed to its own traditions. In particular, this section discusses the fundamental reality that modern feminists seem determined to deny: that some women are bound to be wives and mothers. For all their theorizing, the more radical arm of the feminist wing has never adequately explained how society is supposed to operate successfully if all women completely reject undertaking the social responsibilities that these roles fulfill.

As Betty Friedan elaborated, it is quite understandable that housewives with inquisitive intellects and too much spare time in 1960s America would have liked to exercise their minds on something a little more challenging than another recipe for ground beef and an exciting new window treatment. It is also true that, back in the bad old days, many employers routinely fired women employees when they got married or became pregnant because, as they saw it, being a wife and mother was a full-time job that was completely incompatible with out-of-the-home employment. The feminist movement was justified in opposing those discriminatory, and, in our day, economically unrealistic practices. But many modern feminists have focused upon the institution of marriage, itself, as the means historically employed by men to keep women "down." This is, to state it bluntly, a perverse interpretation. In fact, Betty Friedan herself rebelled against the so-called "Second Wave" of feminism that embraced the wholesale disposal of traditional womanhood, recognizing that the rejection of marriage and family was taking the women's movement to a place that most women likely had no interest in going. But the movement plowed on, insisting that this new view of marriage was the only true route to fulfilled womanhood.

Upon closer inspection, however, the rejection of marriage seems to have been borne primarily out of the private misery of women who had made foolish or unfortunate choices about their marriages and families, or who grew up in households that were less than harmonious. From this, they extrapolated their discontent into a sort of universal injustice against women that could only be alleviated not by pursuing their personal fulfillment, but by lashing back at what they perceived as society's oppressive influences on their personal choices. They were happy to place the blame on these social pressures because it allowed them to deny any personal complicity in the misery in which they found themselves, whether or not they found the alternatives palatable. This dissatisfaction became the essence of the feminist motto: "the personal is the political."

Employing the phrase "the personal is the political" was feminism's means of giving women an "out." By embracing the idea that their own personal situations were merely symptomatic of a society-wide phenomenon, dissatisfied women could avoid accepting responsibility for the choices they made ("it is all society's fault"), and thereby also avoid any guilt from turning their backs on their responsibilities ("I have an obligation to all women to assert myself and break free from this cultural straitjacket"). It was convenient to recast the restrictive social structure as a conspiracy by men to force women into marriage and motherhood by cutting off any other paths to economic well-being and success.

But by sneering at marriage and motherhood, modern feminists fail to appreciate the fact that their own dissatisfaction, by itself, does not demonstrate that these roles are worthless or unimportant. In fact, the opposite can be more forcefully argued: women were channeled into these roles because creating and caring for family was also critically important to society, and merited a priority that was distinct from, and in many ways superior to, merely contributing to the economy. This is not to say that women cannot or should not be anything else. But being a good wife and a good mother is no small accomplishment, and neither is it demeaning. Furthermore, being a good wife does not mean being meek, subservient, and slavish any more than being a good husband means being domineering, stubborn, and insensitive. Taking spousal responsibilities seriously is both personally and socially important, and intelligent husbands and wives the world over have recognized this fact.

In this section on marriage, the conflicts between feminist theory and the persistent reality of marriage are addressed within the following contexts: first, the problems confronted by young women today in trying to develop relationships with men with a view toward marriage; second, the feminist distortion of what marriage means; third, the true meaning of traditional marriage; and, finally, the problems women now face in trying to preserve and uphold marriage in the post-feminist world.

Chapter Six: Forging Lasting Relationships with Men From the Feminist Perspective: Where Idealism and Reality Collide

Men are easy to get but hard to keep.

--Mae West

Virtually no woman raised in America today, or in the last 40 years, can escape the feminist influence on her life. With the possible exception of deeply religious communities, the feminists have defined expectations for modern women that place marriage and motherhood, as ambitions, on a level much lower than professional achievement. Lifelong dedication to a career seems to be the base model for the feminist woman; marriage and children are after-market upgrades. Thus, even women who expressly want marriage and motherhood have been taught to view those roles as adjuncts to their more "defining" roles, which are, theoretically, their involvement in glamorous, challenging, exciting, and demanding careers.

Throughout the 1970's and 1980's, women were becoming fully integrated into the American workforce. Today, the feminist-inspired vision presented to young women is that they are tomorrow's doctors, lawyers, and corporation CEOs. Gone is the stodgy and demeaning 1950's image of the young single office girl (or worse, the spinsterish unmarried middle-aged woman) as an efficient executive secretary who happily quits her dead-end job when she finally gets married. Young women today generally feel that their primary focus should be on going to college and pursuing a profession. And while marriage and family are not ruled out, neither are they given much thought. Having a husband and children is not regarded by many young women as a primary aim of life, and neither are marriage and motherhood considered as legitimate defining roles. Young women are encouraged by feminists to sneer at the idea of giving too much attention to husband-hunting or to their "biological clocks"—even when women candidly admit that they eventually want to marry. As a result, there does not seem to be sufficient serious thought given to what the high-profile career path really means to women, individually, in terms of how professional ambitions are supposed to mesh with other life interests such as relationships, marriage, and family. It seems to be assumed that these additional interests will all simply fall neatly into place. For the most part, women are led to believe that it is a simple logistical proposition.

For the middle-class well-educated female, the pattern of expectations shaped by the feminist ideal is something like this: women should get a college degree, get a good, well-paying job that will allow them to buy their own nice cars, their even nicer stylish, sexy-but-in-good-taste wardrobe, live in their own apartments, pursue a promising career, and casually date a well-filtered stream of intelligent, upwardly mobile, and meticulously-groomed young men. And when women ultimately decide to marry and eventually decide to have children, they will be able to choose from a suitable stable of eligible men, and their husbands will be fully supportive of their career ambitions. Further, while they expect to take a few weeks off when their babies are born, they will then return to work by cheerfully ensconcing their children in a safe, well-run but reasonably-priced day-care facility while they conquer the corporate world. And, of course, husbands will joyfully participate fully in all of the domestic functions of the household: cleaning the house, folding the laundry, cooking the meals, changing, feeding, and bathing the baby, and so on, and the children will happily go along with this whole scheme.

But as luck would have it, this vision has little to do with social and emotional reality, let alone economic reality. Feminism was hopelessly naïve in assuming that, just because women's lives changed, men and children—not to mention women themselves—would automatically adapt to the new reality without any upheaval. Thus, although there may be women whose lives fit into this mold more or less, the conformity is often superficial. Men and women simply do not approach life from the same perspective, and children's needs are another thing altogether. In the end, the optimistically envisioned egalitarian model is not always practical. So while some women may shoehorn their lives into this model, the fit is probably not as seamless as it might appear, nor as satisfying. Ironically, many women have come to find out that the easy part of the picture is working for a paycheck. The hard part is getting married, staying married, and raising a family.

Notwithstanding feminist anti-marriage rhetoric and today's horrendous divorce rate, study after study indicates that single women still want to get married. And precisely because most women *do* want marriage, they eagerly pursue relationships, but fail to appreciate the pitfalls that await them in this post-feminist world. Women engage in destructive patterns of emotional as well as practical behavior, and those patterns repeat themselves constantly. Unmarried women who want to marry tend to fall into two categories. The first is the "old-fashioned" model, and the second is the opposite, the "feminist" model.

The old-fashioned model behaves somewhat like this: when she enters into a serious or even semi-serious relationship, she acts as though this relationship is permanent and operates much like her grandmother's generation . . . but without the social and economic guarantees that marriage (used to) provide. She naively thinks that a real-life demonstration of domestic bliss will win her the prized gold ring. She is apt to put her own professional life into a holding pattern while she simultaneously supports and encourages her boyfriend's ambitions and, even more, caters to and accommodates her boyfriend's interests. Some years later, after the relationship falls apart and the blossom of her youth is waning, she bitterly beats herself up for giving up on her own ambitions. She conveniently concludes that men are pigs, and that the feminists are right. She never chastises herself for her real failing: she did not acknowledge the fact that marriage is marriage . . . and that anything less is not.

Meanwhile, the woman who adopts the "feminist" approach never emotionally commits to a relationship because she does not want it to detract her from focusing on the milestones of her career goals. When she is young, she has no trouble attracting men (who, without expressly admitting it, are ecstatic that she is not interested in marriage). As a result, she believes that an assortment of willing men will be waiting in the wings to marry her when she decides *she is ready* to take that step. She may become so completely self-absorbed that she fails to realize until she is already "past her prime," so to speak, that she would really prefer to come home to something a little warmer than a DVD player. If she encounters trouble finding marriageable men, she is likely to conclude that men only want to marry old-fashioned, submissive women not at all like her. Like the old-fashioned model, she conveniently concludes that men are pigs, and that the feminists are right. She then rededicates herself to her career, consoling herself that married women with children are really miserable and are insanely envious of her success and her freedom.

The truth, however, is something other than what either of these women imagines. The truth is that the feminist movement has done more to liberate single young men from the shackles of mid-20th century social mores than to liberate single young women. Few young men feel any social compulsion to marry. And why not? Most of them are perfectly able to get the benefits of the marital relationship: physical intimacy, emotional support, and even domestic help. But they bear few, or none, of the responsibilities. They don't even have to shoulder the tab as they used to; on the contrary, most women *insist* on paying their way in the post-feminist world. Men aren't tied down to monogamous relationships or even long-term attachments. They can afford to play a waiting game that women cannot. Men can have their cake and eat it, too.

As a result, young women who want to get married (that is, most women) find themselves caught in a crossfire of conflicting inducements. Feminists have tried to convince them that enjoying the pleasures of extra-marital intimacy is emotional satisfaction enough, even when it clearly is not. Feminism ignores or discounts the fact that, quite sensibly, many women want the emotional security that marriage promises, particularly when it comes to their desire to have children. It tries to convince young women that choosing marriage and family amounts to "giving up" their supposedly more meaningful personal ambitions, that they will "lose their identity" if they marry, and that getting married constitutes a betrayal of their sex. Thus, at the same time many women want marriage, they seem to have an irrational and silly fear of it. Women who, quite sensibly, seek a lasting, fulfilling, and good marriage and family life find that feminism has little to offer them in terms of guidance and support. This is a tremendously large oversight of the feminist movement, to put it mildly, given how large a role marriage and motherhood plays in most women's lives.

Neither women nor men can—or should—deny their deeper physiological and emotional desires as inconvenient trivialities. The idea of abolishing marriage may have some superficial and intellectual appeal, but it does not, and really cannot, convince people—men and women alike—into a state of mind that simply eradicates not merely all the urgings of nature and their emotional needs, but the very real limitations that nature and needs place upon them. In essence, by rejecting the validity of marriage, feminism has created a shirt with one sleeve, and told women to accommodate their bodies to the new fashion.

By buying into the feminist perception of marriage, even part of the way, young women engage in a sort of willful blindness, thinking that, as "modern" women, they fully comprehend all of the risks and obligations of relationships in this new post-feminist society. But feminism has never really prepared women for the new reality they helped to create. Under this new social regime, the only sound behavior for women who want marriage and family is to pursue them with committed resolve, intelligence, and discretion, but at the same time to pay heed to establishing and developing their independent economic capabilities. Even women who emphatically want marriage cannot simply plan on marriage or on the economic security of marriage as women used to, because getting married—and staying married—is no longer a social norm. If women fail to establish their economic independence, they risk being both alone *and* financially or professionally stunted. At the same time, women who want marriage "someday" cannot put marriage on a "backburner" while they plan their lives, as though their desires will neatly fall into place on schedule.

In short, young women, while they are still young, need to take an honest assessment of what they want in terms of marriage, family, and career, and to jettison those prejudices that make them approach marriage with fear if they decide that marriage is what they want. And once they decide they do want marriage, they need to take charge of their personal futures through active effort and with their eyes wide open. They should be unapologetic about refusing to waste time and effort on men and relationships in which marriage is not on the table. In the post-feminist culture, marriage will not simply "happen" to women just because women want it to happen. And unfortunately, modern women need to learn how to be comfortable with independence when the marriage and family they want still don't materialize.

Most women (and men) still seek the commitment of marriage, for perfectly sound reasons. There is nothing particularly glamorous or fulfilling about being alone, or about dating an endless stream of varied prospective companions, with the emotional insecurity and unsatisfying open-endedness of impermanency and self-absorption. Although it is a cliché, soon-to-be brides have showers in which their companions gush at the joy of setting up a home and starting a family, and soon-to-be grooms are given bachelor parties in which their companions mourn the loss of their friend's unencumbered lifestyle. Is this all just play-acting? Are men and women so gullible that they can be duped by Madison Avenue advertising executives and bridal magazine publishers into harboring feelings that are entirely counterfeit? Hardly.

These perfectly normal outlooks on marriage are not just the result of customs imposed by oppressive social conditioning. They say something fundamental about the nature of men and women. And while feminists seem to want to convince women that it is "natural," instead, for them to have an aversion to marriage, it is difficult to discern what shred of history or biology that belief could possibly be based upon. The fact is, it is usually women who seek the commitment of marriage for the simple reason that the idea of family promises an emotional fulfillment that cannot be satisfied in any other way. There is really no reason to believe that a majority of the women of yesteryear were any less eager to enter into marriage than are the women of today. Most women—and most men—still want what marriage represents.

The feminist movement has never conceded the dreadful impact on many women of its position on marriage. In dismissing and diminishing it, the feminists are ignoring the fact that pursuing professional interests within (and not *against*) a relationship is a reality for most women, and women, whether seeking marriage or already married, simply cannot (and *should* not) ignore the importance of marriage when pursuing their professional and personal ambitions. The ironic part of the feminists' position is that they are enforcing essentially the same standard that existed right up through the 1960s: a woman may pursue a career *or* a family, but she cannot have both. While the challenges of pursuing both are admittedly difficult, this time around, women are being told that they will be better off by making marriage the casualty, not career. Yet reality does not seem to confirm the wisdom of that proposition.

Again, it is easy to sympathize with Betty Friedan's frustrated housewives. Furthermore, it is surely true that there were plenty of truly bad marriages—that is, ones in which a spouse was abusive or perennially unfaithful—that were held together by social and economic forces, and it is easy to decry such things as outmoded and cruel. But for many women, being a wife and mother was, and is, a perfectly viable and satisfying role, no matter what the feminists say. What was to blame, as the early women's movement recognized, was the lack of any *other* outlet in which women could invest themselves. Today, those outlets exist, but the feminists have exalted those diversions over marriage to the point that marriage is now seen as incidental to a woman's other life goals. For many women, this is precisely backwards.

Yet, one fact must be conceded. From their perspective, the feminists' persistence in deriding marriage is perfectly understandable. It is because they have little concept of what marriage is, or ought to be, or even could be.

Chapter Seven: Feminism's Perspective on Marriage

Since marriage constitutes slavery for women, it is clear that the Women's Movement must concentrate on attacking this institution. Freedom for women cannot be won without the abolition of marriage.

--Sheila Cronan

Patricia Ireland, when she was the president of NOW, once gave a speech explaining part of her transformation into becoming a strident feminist. In recounting her experiences in law school, she learned in her first-year Property class that women used to be regarded as property, and that is one of the reasons that women bore their husband's names. To signify her rejection of this oppressive legal regime, she determined to retain her own name. Did the irony never strike her that she was thereby retaining the name of her . . . father? But more than that, since the law no longer treats women as property, what did *she* intend her name retention to signify? After all, while it is easy to understand why a woman might want to retain her name if she has a certain level of name-recognition or it will cause confusion, are names really all that critical in terms of self-identity?

It is very easy to understand why women would rebel against the idea of being treated as property. At the same time, however, identifying a woman by reference to her father or husband would be utterly necessary and critical to the welfare of women under such a legal regime. In a legal world where women have little or no independent status, and are treated, initially, as the property of their fathers, and later, as property of their husbands, the adoption of the husband's name provided women with legal protection, such as it was. In identifying themselves as belonging to someone, it protected women from the advances or claims or force of others who might attempt to exercise dominion. Thus, however much one may justly decry the idea of women as property, the convention of taking on one's husband's name was a perfectly sound and rational legal development that served a valid purpose—a purpose, moreover, that protected women from even more dire consequences than being treated as property. It seems rather silly, then, to make more of the form than the function. Today, retaining one's "own" name as a form of protest seems a little feeble.

What is more, the idea of identifying one's self with the name of one's closest relations has never been reserved exclusively to women being treated as property. Almost every culture has created name identities that go far beyond the marital relationship. Name prefixes and suffixes like "Mc" and "O'" or von or van and so on specifically derived from identifying one's relationship to other people, usually one's father, and, from there, to one's extended family or clan. In Japan, for example, where one can hardly claim that its cultural traditions have pioneered women's rights, men occasionally took their wife's name upon marrying if the wife came from a particularly prominent family. So: what did Ms. Ireland truly intend by choosing to reject an identifier that would signal, to the world, her relationship to her own husband?

As stated above, women may choose to retain their own names for various reasons. But in the case of women who choose to do so purely out of a conscious feminist-inspired effort to retain some "independent" identity from their spouses, one has to wonder: what does that signify about the meaning of their marriage to them? Is it truly the joining of two people to form an undivided whole, and, if so, why would it be desirable to identify oneself to the world as distinct from that union? The question is not posed because there is a ready answer. It is posed because the issue of name retention manifestly begs the question. After all, if a woman, through marriage, expresses her willingness to share a home, bank account, children, the remainder of her life, an assortment of bodily fluids, and a host of other things, is a name just too . . . personal?

Today, when divorce is rampant, the conclusion is unavoidable that marriage means something vastly different than what it meant a century ago, and for the many centuries preceding it. This is true, of course, whether or not one credits that change to the emancipation of women or to some other factor. But the idea of retaining a "separate identity" is symptomatic of a mindset that undermines *true* marriage in fundamental ways. In many respects, one might claim that what is called marriage today is not marriage at all, but simply a legal arrangement. And, judging by some of the feminist articles that discuss marriage, this appears to be the extent of the meaning of marriage; in fact, the legal aspect is just about the only thing that seems to *recommend* marriage to many feminists. When one takes a look at the push by feminists and others to grant to homosexual couples the right to "marry," for example, it is abundantly clear that all they are really interested in is a bundle of legal rights and obligations, a contract mutually agreed upon by two people bound by their affection and sexual attraction. What is more, they seem to think that marriage should last only so long as it benefits either party, to be cancelled unilaterally by either party whenever it fails to meet either party's expectations. Is that all marriage is?

It appears to be, to some feminists. One telling glimpse into a feminist perspective on marriage may be gleaned from the women who defended former President Bill Clinton during the Monica Lewinsky scandal.

To refresh your memory (with apologies), the whole matter came about as a result of a lawsuit filed by Paula Jones against Bill Clinton when he was the President. Ms. Jones claimed that, when she was a state employee in Arkansas, she was taken up to see the then-Governor of Arkansas, who proceeded to disrobe and invite Ms. Jones to partake in some extra-curricular recreation. Ms. Jones refused, and, after being darkly encouraged to remain silent, left. One expects that this would all have been kept under a hat as an amusing little anecdote, except for a news item which came out a few years later when Clinton became President. In the article, a former Arkansas state trooper told a story of how he had obtained a woman named "Paula" for an informal assignation with the Governor in a hotel suite, and that this "Paula" had happily complied. This besmirching of her honor, it is to be presumed (generously), prompted Paula Jones to file a harassment suit against the President.

In the ensuing proceedings, it came out that Clinton had had an affair with a 23-year old White House intern named Monica Lewinsky and tried to cover it up by both lying about it in his own deposition, and by asking Ms. Lewinsky to lie about it in hers. There is an assortment of other details that emerged, but suffice it to say that it became apparent that the President had a distasteful habit of behaving himself like a dime-store Don Juan.

As president, Clinton's political stances were directly in line with the feminists' political agenda; consequently, it is easy to understand why they did not want him to be impeached. So while they poked fun at the impeachment proceedings because it was "just about sex," few stepped forward to express any offense or outrage. Instead, most reacted with disappointment, at best, or mild condemnation, at worst. (To be fair, one Virginia chapter of NOW did condemn him soundly, so much so that it expressed its willingness to break off from NOW completely for not being as uncompromising in its stance.)

In an attempt to bolster feminism's credibility, Gloria Steinem, in an editorial in the New York Times, pointed out that there was a great distinction between Clinton's behavior and the behavior of Bob Packwood (a Senator who had been forced to resign over his grotesque habit of pawing women indiscriminately) and Clarence Thomas (discussed previously), particularly regarding Clinton's treatment of Monica Lewinsky: "Welcome sexual behavior is about as relevant to sexual harassment as borrowing a car is to stealing one." And she was right, as far as that goes. Ms. Steinem seemed to think that the really important thing to understand about the President was that he knew that no meant no, and yes meant yes. Thus, when he propositioned Paula Jones, it was okay because he did not force himself on her, and when he indulged Monica Lewinsky, it was okay because she wanted to do it. Consequently, she argued, it was perfectly understandable that feminists would continue to stand by him, and there was no reason for them not to:

> For one thing, if the President had behaved with comparable insensitivity toward environ-mentalists, and at the same time remained their most vocal champion and bulwark against an

anti-environmental Congress, would they be
expected to desert him? I don't think so.

By this statement, one is to understand that Clinton's behavior
merely demonstrated "insensitivity" to the concerns of feminists
about harassment and respect, but was not sufficiently momentous
to make them actually turn their backs on him.

Columnist Maureen Dowd recounted that Patricia Ireland
conceded that the situation was a tough one for NOW, and quoted
her as saying:

> It's harder for us to deal with the bad behavior
> and bad treatment of women by men who stand
> with us on policy. We've been getting a lot of e-
> mails and phone calls from women saying:
> "How can you go after Clinton? He's appointed
> more women, blah-blah-blah." . . . You can be a
> womanizer, and, yes, even women can find that
> attractive . . . I keep wanting to turn to him and
> say, "Grow up."

Grow up, indeed. Yet, what both Gloria, Patricia, and
their allies conveniently neglected to address was: what about
Hillary? Does yes mean yes, no mean no, and infidelity mean . . .
nothing? You see, Ms. Steinem was mostly correct that Bill's
behavior with respect to various and sundry women—Kathleen
Willey, Gennifer Flowers, Monica Lewinsky, Paula Jones—really
was not particularly interesting or important except for one fact:
he was married. And there's the rub. Bill's marriage to Hillary
and fatherhood of Chelsea are the *only* important facts of his
otherwise boorish behavior. (That is, important in terms of
marriage. The fact that he was willing to expose the presidency to

such indignity says something else.) They were the reason he had to have his state troopers quietly usher women to his hotel suites, the reason Paula Jones was encouraged to be silent, the reason he lied in his deposition, and the reason he asked Monica Lewinsky to lie. Had President Clinton been a single man, none of his earthy habits would have mattered. The issue was not "just sex," the issue was the hypocrisy of his gross infidelity: what sort of man claims to sympathize with the plight of women railing against patriarchal oppression, then treats the most important women in his life with such contemptible disregard?

Feminists acted as though Hillary and Chelsea did not exist. But the fact remains that Hillary (and to a degree, Chelsea) was the reason the scandal was a scandal at all; Hillary was the elephant in the room that feminists ignored. She and her marriage were, unfortunately for her, political irrelevancies to "more important" interests: abortion, healthcare, equal pay, and so on. One pro-choice journalist remarked that she would happily have provided sexual favors to the President to thank him for keeping abortion legal, and a Democrat woman lawmaker asked "Why couldn't he just keep it in his pants for eight years so he could get something done?" Eight lousy years? By the time the Lewinsky scandal broke, the Clintons had been married for 22 years.

Of course, some feminists, perhaps a bit sheepishly, tried to gloss over the marriage aspect by claiming that what happened within the Clinton family was their own business. True enough. But that position was in itself a turnabout: what happened to "the personal is the political"? Other women who found themselves in precisely the same position as Hillary were told that their own indignation was not merely personal, but a political awakening to the just cause of feminism. But in Hillary's case, the political was most emphatically the political and, by the way, completely and totally unrelated to the personal.

While groups like NOW were careful to condemn the idea that men should not use the "aphrodisiac of power" to awe young, impressionable women into bestowing sexual favors, they were also careful to describe Clinton's affair with Monica as "consensual"—as if all that really mattered in this shameful spectacle was Monica's frame of mind. In the end, even Hillary was cornered into jumping on the bandwagon, feebly explaining her decision to let it ride: "He was not only my husband, he was my president." In many ways, that seemed to say it all. But what else could Hillary do? Nobody really stood up for her: not her would-be feminist allies, and certainly not the opposition who disagreed with her on everything. Even Hillary's statement was not a defense of marriage *as* marriage; it was an excuse for marriage. For Hillary, it was either stick with her husband, or lose both personally and politically. And while one cannot contend that Bill's behavior should have necessitated Hillary's filing for divorce, one is left wondering: why didn't anyone stand up for marriage? Was the President's behavior the sort of respect and regard the feminists believe husbands should show their wives as equal partners?

Even more pointedly: was the feminists' behavior the sort of respect and regard that women should show for other women? They seemed to think it helped their case to cast the President's offense (which they discounted at any rate) as having nothing whatsoever to do with his treatment of his own wife, but rather with his treatment of *other* women. But that treatment was to use them for pleasure and dispose of them like so much plastic dinnerware. And as Maureen Dowd astutely pointed out, the lack of outrage shown by feminists partially stemmed from the fact that they happily and cattily treated Clinton's women with the same amount of disdain as he did because they were "NOCD": "not our class, dear." What feminists never owned up to is the fact that they utterly failed to uphold the honor or dignity of *either* Hillary *or* Bill's motley harem—or any other real woman. Instead, they stood up for a fifty-something lecher who treated both his ambitious, smart, career-oriented wife and his more colorful women on the side with the same despicable callousness.

Universally, feminists seemed to discuss only the issue of harassment, never marital infidelity. This in itself was a peculiar preoccupation, since the impeachment charge against President Clinton had *nothing to do with harassment*, but included perjury and obstruction of justice—specifically, *his attempts to cover up his infidelity*. By being so preoccupied with their political tight-rope act on harassment, groups like NOW implicitly endorsed the idea that it is perfectly okay for men to behave like scoundrels with respect to women. As one male commentator pointed out, what's the point of being an alpha male if you can't take advantage of it? President Clinton was completely relieved of all the burdens of marriage that traditionally fall upon men: he did not have to be a breadwinner (on the contrary, feminists touted the fact that Hilary always made more money than he did); he did not have to be a doting and dedicated husband and father; he did not have to be the protector of the family; he did not have to be faithful. He did not even have to be *there*. Rather than step up to defend himself when the scandal broke loose, he retreated behind the veil of his office and sent out his wife and his female Secretary of State, Madeline Albright, to defend his honor in public, but only because the first ploy of asking a 23 year-old female intern to lie for him failed.

One can only imagine the great number of "old boys" who were secretly gleeful about the whole spectacle, scoffing at

Hillary's tragic and inexcusable humiliation while Bill scampered about with an assortment of disposable women: "You've got to love a woman who doesn't mind her husband playing around with floosies on the side, eh? What a trooper!" And as the feminists conceded, plenty of women, even some of those self-same feminists, were more than willing to line up to feed Clinton's unappetizing appetite for meaningless sexual trysts. Even Clinton must have been amazed. Notwithstanding the fact that he treated virtually all the women who surrounded him without an ounce of respect, he couldn't lose. The President discovered the Mother Lode: in return for supporting abortion, nationalized healthcare, and a host of other hot-button feminist political issues, the feminists would happily and unapologetically grant him a license to exploit any woman he wanted to his heart's (and other bodily organs') content.

The Clintons' marriage, as marriages go, does not exhibit any unheard of characteristics (unfortunately), but it is illustrative because it ended up smack dab at the intersection of modern feminist politics and traditional marriage. Hillary was feminism's original cause incarnate: a capable, bright, accomplished woman married to a man who was apparently not threatened by her strength and who was supposedly sympathetic to everything feminism stood for. Yet what did the Clintons exemplify that feminism may now boast of? To millions of women in America, Bill did not represent the ideal model of a man, let alone a husband, and Hillary hardly represented the sort of woman they wanted to emulate. Yet strangely, feminists failed to fully comprehend why so many women were disgusted with President Clinton and, in turn, with them—and it had nothing to do with the issue of harassment. To decent people everywhere, the hypocrisy inherent in the situation was somewhat repulsive. Is this really what feminism stands for?

Yet, after all the brouhaha, Hillary became the darling of the feminists; they were staunchly behind her run for the presidency in 2008. As Maureen Dowd explained it, Hillary's popularity and electability emerged "only when she played the doormat card." Yet after blithely dismissing her husband's infidelity as a trivial inconvenience, one almost wonders how Hillary was able to stomach the feminists' support.

To any woman who takes marriage seriously, Bill Clinton is something of a buffoon, notwithstanding the fact that he was the President of the United States. And this is Hillary's unfortunate dilemma. Few other strong, intelligent women would have tolerated his frat-boy infidelities in a husband, particularly given their highly public character. It must have been tremendously difficult for Hillary to act dignified in the face of such juvenile misconduct. Certainly, generations of women were told that their self-respect and self-worth demanded that they refuse to tolerate it. But in the world of modern feminism, Clinton's personal behavior was not nearly as important as his political power. And because the Clintons were politically tied to the feminists, for Hillary, whatever marriage might have meant to her, it had to be subsumed to a greater cause, a greater aspiration. Any betrayal she may have felt for herself and for her daughter was relegated to an inferior concern. To a large degree, the only course left for her was to act as though her marriage, *as marriage*, was not as important as other matters, regardless of what she may have felt personally, regardless of what choices she might have made had her life not been inside of a political fish-bowl. She could only maintain her own dignity by undermining the dignity of marriage. Once again: he was not just her husband, he was her President.

It is hard to understand the relationship between Bill and Hillary Clinton, and, truly, understanding it is not really anyone else's business. But what is interesting is that most of America has assumed that their marriage is primarily a political bargain. It is highly likely that it is much more than that, but why is that the common wisdom? Simple: because of Bill's chronic infidelity. And that's the point: most of America thinks that marriage, at a minimum, ought to include fidelity; ergo, their marriage must be something else.

As a political partnership, the Clinton marriage has worked tremendously well. Bill may have been immature, unfaithful, and single-mindedly ambitious, but he is not stingy. Hillary is also ambitious, which is why Bill's infidelity was seen by others only as a bothersome inconvenience insofar as it detracted from their political mission. Aided by her own considerable efforts, intellect, experience, reputation, and energies, Hillary was able to take advantage of her husband's early political success to earn seats on high-profile corporate boards and bring in lucrative clients to the Rose Law Firm and, for herself, good earnings and prestige at that same firm. She used her considerable savvy to help win for Bill the presidency and for herself a stint as First Lady. Afterward, she was able to take advantage of her fame and victimhood to catapult herself into the political spotlight to become first, a Senator; second, the first truly viable woman presidential candidate in United States history; and third, Secretary of State (it is okay to be *that* kind of secretary). So while Hillary traipses around the world, her husband Bill carries on with whatever he is doing with his foundation. They may even see each other now and then. And yes, Hillary will be written up in the history books. So: what about marriage?

One is left to conclude that, as far as the feminists are concerned, the Clinton marriage represents the pinnacle of marital aspirations. It is a marriage that satisfactorily answers the only question they consider relevant: "what's in it for me?" –leaving out all considerations of the well-being and integrity of the union itself. But very few women believe that, for want of a better description, a "Clinton" type of marriage is a respectable, legitimate, or even desirable object of marriage: simply to be the next political / corporate / Hollywood "power couple," and to heck with all the staid old conventions like fidelity, commitment, intimacy, sacrifice, love, respect, children, and actually living with and spending time with your spouse. Most women do not regard their marriages primarily or exclusively as a tool for economic, political, or professional enhancement. And this is precisely why the feminists, as a rule, do not fully comprehend the meaning of marriage.

Chapter Eight: "I Do" is Supposed to Really Mean "I Do"

A successful marriage requires falling in love many times, always with the same person.

--Mignon McLaughlin

Worldly success may be what many women want; it may even be what some ambitious women marry for. But it is hardly the purpose for the institution of marriage.

What positive things do feminists have to offer women today in support of marriage *as* marriage? What have they done to improve and strengthen marriage for the millions of women who are already married or who want to get married, to encourage spouses to respect and honor one another? How have they empowered women to build their marriages and families so that the necessary support is there for these women to become leaders in business, politics, and society, yet still have the fulfillment of stable families, loving husbands, and happy, well-cared for children?

As a movement . . . very little. For example, clear back to 1996, NOW's only activism on behalf of marriage has been to seek to extend its "benefits" to homosexual couples. And the reason the word "benefits" is here in quotes is that the feminists otherwise do not seem to have much use for marriage, let alone believe it offers any benefits. Otherwise, NOW has little to say about marriage beyond a few short statements on adultery: consistent with the Clinton debacle, they play it down. Of course, no one with any sense, let alone a sense of justice, would defend the Islamic custom of stoning women who commit adultery, so no one can fault NOW's condemnation of the practice, but why is that the extent of NOW's conjugal concerns? NOW's only other mention of adultery is its opposition to the unequal enforcement of the United States Military Code against adulterers, by which women are generally treated more harshly than men. In that, they clearly have a point . . . except that their response is to defend female officers found guilty of the offense, rather than to seek condemnation of the men who are similarly guilty, but get off with a mere slap on the wrist. While it is easy to decry the discrimination aspect, one cannot help but ask: is adultery really no big deal? And if they really think that, have they arrived at that opinion by asking any married couples?

Let's backtrack a little. For nostalgic reasons, if for nothing else, it is helpful to recap some traditional marriage vows (give or take a few conditions). This is, traditionally, what the celebrant asks of each spouse, and to which each spouse must assent in order to effect the marriage:

> Will you love (him/her), comfort (him/her), honor and keep (him/her), in sickness and in health, for richer, for poorer, for better, for worse, in sadness and in joy, to love and to cherish, forsaking all others, keep yourself only unto (him/her) as long as you both shall live?

This is not a casual vow. It says "forsaking all others" and "keep yourself only unto him/her." It also says "as long as you both shall live," not, "for the time being, anyway" or "until something better comes along," or "until I have just had enough and cannot take it anymore because I need to find myself." And it is not just for health and for richer and for better and for joy, but actually applies when matters do not turn out so well.

Arguably, there is no single greater or more important act in most people's lives than the taking of a marriage vow. This is why so many people spend a fortune on weddings—it is not simply an excuse for a big party. The importance of marriage is precisely why a wedding *is* a party, to which couples generally invite all of their family members, their friends, and their colleagues: everyone becomes a witness to the couple's promises. When the celebrant asks whether anyone present at the ceremony knows any reason why the bride and groom should not be joined, silence constitutes an endorsement of the marriage, as well as a tacit agreement to recognize and support it.

There are meanings behind most of the traditions within a wedding ceremony, and there are reasons that a wedding is a wedding. The customs are not arbitrary or just so much fluff and pomp. But whether the bride and groom opt for all the traditions, or instead reject them as antiquated and sexist, the key for any married couple is the moment they say "I do" or "I will." In that instant, whatever motivations or ambitions or interests guided their behavior in the past must necessarily succumb to a superseding governing interest: the union. This is called a "commitment," not enslavement. "Enslavement" merely appears to be radical feminist shorthand for "Reset. I did not realize I had to mean what I said. In any case, I changed my mind."

When an individual, man or woman, decides to marry, he or she is expressing the greatest possible statement of love, faith, and hope. Couples willingly, happily, and voluntarily agree, usually at a fairly young age, to bind their lives to one another until death, to pledge their futures to someone they have, in many cases, only known for a few years. They promise themselves to another person who is totally unrelated to them, to someone who does not have, by any natural obligation, any reason other than love and will to look out for and promote their interests.

No one knows what the future holds other than what people control by their own actions. Consequently, when you really stop to think about it, it is astounding that the same people who have trouble choosing what color sofa to buy seem to have little or no trouble assenting to marriage. And if more people gave really serious, rational, and considered thought to what they were actually promising, one wonders that anyone would get married at all. This is probably why the parents of the bride and groom tend to worry about the marriage more than the bride and groom. Yet people get married every day.

But also, today, many of those marriages are ending in divorce. And while one cannot discount the reality that there may be grave reasons for one spouse to seek a divorce—chronic infidelity, physical abuse, drug or alcohol addiction, and so on—these represent a small subset of the divorces that occur. Too often, there is no other explanation for divorce than the fact that individuals seeking them would rather be craven and selfish than courageous, optimistic, and industrious by living up to their vows, even though they usually describe their behavior with nicer sounding phrases. The real key to marriage is that "voluntary" aspect. In the marriage vow, a spouse promises to put the marriage first, and the self second (or lower), until one of them dies. And it is most emphatically *not* something society forces the couple to do, no matter what feminists might argue. They do it themselves.

It is not just on the wedding day that the vow matters. In some respects, that is the least critical day of any marriage. The vow binds a couple into the future; the vow says they will do what they said they would do every single day. The vow means that from that point forward, the decisions a couple makes are made together, and for the benefit of the marriage and the family, not for "me." Through the carrying out of that vow, the spouses actually become greater than themselves; the union becomes an entity distinct from the two individuals who create it.

In a true marriage, all the carrying on about "losing your identity" is just so much counterculture nonsense. Once men and women take the vow, they either live up to it or betray it. If their "independent identity" is more important than their marriage, then they should be content to live with their identity, but it is beyond unreasonable to expect their spouses to. The notion that a woman "loses herself" in marriage is valid, but the whole point is: you are *supposed* to lose yourself. Otherwise, why get married? Giving up your preoccupation with yourself is intended to be a good thing, and it *is* a good thing to the couples who truly work at it and succeed. Besides, anyone who has lived with and for themselves long enough should realize that it's not really all it's cracked up to be. Certainly, it is sometimes fun to eat what and when you want, to stay up all night, and to have no one else eat the last of the ice cream or leave their smelly socks in the closet. But so what? The point of life is not to make everything easy. There are many ways to achieve "easy," but they are not particularly interesting or soul-fulfilling or exciting.

The truth is, most people are not very easy to get along with day after day, week in and week out. They can be a real pain, sometimes. But the person you love is also your greatest joy, and if couples work hard at their marriages, the joy is most of the time, and that joy permeates their lives, even on the days that are bad. Every rough day has to be the day that marriage vows are renewed and reinvigorated; those are the days when a spouse is tempted to think of "me" and not of "us." But it is that *willing* act of giving up personal interests that helps the marriage work, and makes the marriage relationship develop into something greater, something that is much more than the sum of its parts.

Every time one encounters spousal malcontents, one has to wonder why they think marriage, alone of all endeavors, and assuredly one of the most important in any person's life, is supposed to be effortless in order to be considered "successful." Almost every other important goal in life is expected to be challenging and difficult; in fact, the more difficult the hurdles, the greater the feeling of accomplishment and the greater the sense of reward and satisfaction. Yet this same approach is too rarely applied to marriage. For some reason, people idealize romantic love and assume that it can easily withstand any assault by the practical and mundane realities of day-to-day living and the occasional misfortune. They treat romantic love as something that happens *to* them, as though they are merely passive victims of love, and not willing participants. This is absurd.

Anything that is important is worth working at, and marriage is no different. In fact, the love a husband and wife share is supposed to sustain the work, and make it clear just why they are making the effort. The recollection of vows is to remind them that they *promised* to make the effort, no matter how tough or uncomfortable or inconvenient or painful or frustrating. It is that giving out of love, out of a promise that may have been made decades in the past, that takes a married couple beyond their parochial and petty and immediate resentments and moods and gripes, that pushes those things into the background of what it is they are trying to attain for themselves and for their family. In that way, marriage becomes an achievement (if that is not too crass a term). Marriage becomes an expression of the best people that these two individuals can become, because they have pushed themselves beyond the narrow limits of their own selfish interests.

Why is the beauty and nobility of this effort so difficult to understand for feminists? For a group of people who always seem to think women need to engage in activism, what is more activist than to truly give yourself for the welfare of another person and for the cause of a successful marriage? The answer is that they don't really mean actual giving, and especially not if it involves a man. Feminist activists like the kind of giving that is comfortable or impersonal, like hanging out with the sisterhood in front of the White House carrying a sign and chanting, or flying to Calcutta for two weeks to "experience" a different culture and to donate some time off to a pet cause. But the reality is that just trying to get along for one solid week with an irritating brother-in-law as a house guest would be much more personally challenging and truly selfless.

The reason most feminists are not interested in accepting the burdens of duty and responsibility that marriage entails is not because marriage is demeaning, but because it is difficult. The exaltation of an "independent identity" is simply an excuse for discarding these difficulties in favor of the ease of selfishness. By giving in to the temptation, they are only conceding their own weakness. Marriage is about selflessness, and it takes a strong person to be selfless. Instead of seeing marriage as a question of willingness, however, feminists prefer to view marriage as a sort of competitive sport, a power struggle. If the man does not give in to what his wife wants because he wants things to be a certain way, he fulfills the role of an oppressor. If the man does give in to what his wife wants, it is a successful marriage, because then it is "equal."

It seems as though, from the feminist perspective, husbands and wives should divvy up their chores and responsibilities and earning power between them with the precision of a corporate merger, bartering back and forth with one another and taking turns doing the dishes and the cooking. And, in order to retain "self-respect," wives should refuse to "give" anything of themselves without first making sure that they are going to get something out of it that is just as good or better. Presumably, this method of scoring also includes tallying up the amount of money each party earns and contributes to the "partnership."

But marriage is not, primarily, an economic arrangement (however much divorces may be). Marriages are not made "better" by imposing upon them an unwritten rule that each spouse must give equally and take equally, with neither party allowed to collect any unearned benefits. And while it might be desirable for the rest of the world to operate by reference to some unifying economic principle of fairness or equality, that idea is entirely foreign to *what a marriage is,* even if a married couple may freely choose to conform their own marriage to such an idea.

A marriage, and, by extension, a family, is a single unit, and should operate as a single unit. A family is the ideal cooperative venture. Thus, the little baby, who contributes smiles and laughter and joy and endless love (but no money) should receive all the milk and holding and cuddling and rocking he wants and needs. Older children contribute here and there with their love and funny phrases and silly antics and the occasional picking up of toys and setting the table (but again, no money), and consume a lot of resources in the way of food and clothing and toy-purchasing and story-telling and question-answering and hugs and tuckings-in. And the parents work their tails off keeping the whole affair running as smoothly as they can, contributing laundry-washing, bathing, kisses and hugs, taking care of the house, money-earning, knee-bandaging, bicycle-riding-teaching, sandwich making, juice-getting, and so on between the two of them, and trying now and then to fit in a few favors for one another as well. And the reason a family should work successfully together is not because its aim is to achieve economic efficiency and optimization, but because families are bound by love, and a married couple is easily motivated to give to each other and to their children out of love what they would not be inclined to give without it.

Marriage must be a partnership in the truest sense: a giving of oneself for the good of the union, because the benefits to be derived—emotionally and spiritually (and, from that, usually in many other ways)—from it are so far beyond the silly nitpicking concerns of who-earns-what, who-did-what, who-owes-what, and so on. This is not to say that married couples must embrace all forms of traditional role-playing; in fact, one of the beauties of marriage is that it is self-governed. So if wives feel put-upon, one must ask: what is stopping them from working out a solution with their spouses—you know, the men they loved enough to marry? They need not imagine that the meaning of being a "good wife" is as crabbed, stunted, and "patriarchal" as some feminists would have them believe.

Furthermore, if the truth were told, many couples might concede that they actually *prefer* adhering to traditional roles, even when they pretend to disdain them. For every woman who complains about how her husband does not do the dishes or the laundry or change the baby enough, half the reason is probably that women refuse to cede authority over these household chores to their husbands. At the same time that they may not always enjoy them, they exercise dominion over them because, underneath, they believe their husbands are not as good as they are (or just plain incompetent) at performing them. So for women who roll their eyes at how poorly their husbands load the dishwasher or fold the laundry, it seems enormously silly to fret over who is doing the dishes on a given night.

Many married women undertake a lot of the traditional "housewife" chores not because they harbor any particular notions that these tasks constitute "women's work." They do them simply because the chores will not do themselves; consequently, there does not seem to be much point in griping about having to get them done. All too often, feminists bog themselves down into complaining about such silly preoccupations. Is having to do the dishes really such an ordeal? Especially when one stops to consider that many husbands undertake traditional men's chores, such as mowing lawns, washing and maintaining cars, fixing fences, and so on. There is no reason on earth that women (let alone men) have to view the chores of running a household as drudgery. These tasks are not about economics, equity, status, and pay scales. They are about contributing to the well-being of the family by making the house and yard nice and clean and making the family content and comfortable. At the end of the day, marriage is not about tallying up what everyone has done and comparing notes to make sure no one got an unfair advantage. Marriage demands that couples be grateful to one another for shouldering and sharing these burdens together, not complaining about their share or complaining that these burdens exist. And while it can be quite difficult to work through all these tasks and trials, and while married couples may frequently have disagreements about what to do and how to do it and when to do it and who ought to do it, they should never need to question *why* they are doing it.

By accepting the responsibilities and duties of marriage, however, some feminists claim that married women are "betraying" other women. If a married women is not willing to discard those difficult or unpleasant tasks that nevertheless make her husband and family happy, if she is not *more* interested in being a better lawyer or better accountant or better anything else than in being a better wife and a better mother, feminism characterizes her as subservient or weak, or treats her as if her contributions to the world are miniscule or valueless. However, the contributions of time, effort, and love that go into a content and loving home are incredibly meaningful to the families that receive them, and that judgment is, in the end, worth significantly more than the judgment of feminism or the judgment of history books.

Contrary to the radical feminist perspective, the woman who derives satisfaction from her success and her contributions within the four walls of her home is not wallowing in "ignorance" of her "enslaved" state, and neither is she, as feminist Linda Hirshman supposes, living a "lesser" life than the woman who rejects it for a life with more worldly benefits or attention. If feminism, as an ideology, is to allow for the fact that women may be different from one another, it must allow that a woman whose life is fulfilled by being a wife or mother measures her own value on a different scale—a scale of small, intimate, non-economic, and non-political judgments. It is a scale that rejects all of the "patriarchal" standards—such as money, title, and influence—that the feminists, ironically, frequently measure other women by. It is a scale in which sensibilities matter more than dollars. Besides, even a moment's reflection makes one fact obvious to any thinking person, feminist or otherwise: the importance and influence of a loving home cannot be underestimated.

Individual women do not "owe" to other women the obligation to behave in any particular way. Yet the feminists, for the most part, continue to refuse to countenance women who wholeheartedly embrace marriage and motherhood with joy and self-assurance. This is why they cannot claim to represent either women as a group, or liberation as a concept. It is what is so ridiculous, ultimately, about their position: they are just as adamant about imposing their values on women as the most oppressive patriarchal culture that ever gifted a toaster at a bridal shower. The feminists' idea of "liberated" womanhood does not seem to be liberated at all; instead, it is just shackled by a new set of rigid standards.

Chapter Nine: Well, Where Does That Leave Marriage, Today?

Love seems the swiftest, but it is the slowest of all growths. No man or woman really knows what perfect love is until they have been married a quarter of a century.

--Mark Twain

For some reason, within the modern feminist world, choosing to be a wife (and, usually, mother) full-time is graded as though it is a career. As such, it *is* somewhat of a dead end; being a wife does not have a lot of upward mobility all by itself, even if it may have considerable benefits. But more importantly, being a wife is most emphatically *not* a "career." It is much more.

There is a reason most people get married, and it has nothing whatsoever to do with "getting ahead" or "empowerment." Life is about finding and nurturing those pursuits and relationships that bring us joy and fulfillment. Some women may derive that from a career, some may find it in charity work, some may discover it through their children, and some may obtain it in politics or activism. But many people, men and women alike, find that a good marriage is *a* (if not *the*) key element to their happiness, and that says a great deal about them: it is a testament to their true selflessness.

A good marriage has nothing to do with public, worldly success and everything to do with private, personal success. In that sense, it is bordering on the absurd (to say the least) for the feminists to treat the *relationship* itself as a public policy issue, let alone a feminist issue. The value that a man and a woman place upon their own marriage is really no one else's business.

The *institution* of marriage, however, is everyone's business. It is downright ludicrous to contend that, simply because some women have failed at marriage or found it wanting (or for that matter, never experienced it), it therefore has no use or value to *any* women. Do modern feminists really believe that all the women who came before them were fools?

It is true that marriage may not be useful to women who live and breathe feminism; if so, let them avoid it. But for women who revere and cherish it, feminism's scorn rings rather hollow. The condemnation of marriage is, essentially, a condescension, a boast that one group of people knows better than everyone else how people ought to design their lives. But most human beings, women included, are rational and quite capable of determining their own interests. Given that marriage, today, is a matter that is freely chosen by sound-minded adult men and women, there is no earthly reason for feminists to denigrate the institution of marriage itself simply because they cannot force other people to adapt it to their way of thinking, or lack the imagination to realize that it can be (within reasonable limits) whatever the spouses choose to make of it. Marriage is not about women and men in the abstract, it is about man and woman in the particular.

To revisit the siren call, "the personal is the political," what the feminists fail to acknowledge is that, while the personal may have some political aspect, it also nevertheless remains the personal. In the end, by transferring their personal gripes about marriage into a political cause, feminism opened the door for women to avoid the difficulties and challenges that the personal presents. Resenting men in the abstract is simply the feminists' way of copping out of the need for women to relate to actual men in the real world. Assuredly, the least effective way to learn to deal with men, either in the abstract or in the particular, is by running as far away from them as possible, and then to dehumanize them as much as women claim that men dehumanize them. Life is not really about advancing a cause; frequently, it is simply a struggle to find out what it is that we actually want and to work towards achieving it. And while marriage is a difficult proposition, overcoming the struggles that lead to marital success are what make it infinitely worthwhile.

To appreciate the value of marriage, one need only redirect the discussion to a correlative matter: what alternatives to marriage are there, and are they any better? That is, better for actual people, not better in the service of some bizarre theory. The fact is, there is no alternative in terms of relationships: nothing permanent, nothing committed, nothing pledged. For millions of women, the lack of experiencing a spouse's enduring love and companionship cannot be made up by (cannot even be remotely approached by) evenings in front of cable television, engaging in social activism, hosting stimulating dinner parties, and indulging in casual sex with a series of impermanent associations. It is enough to make you cry: is that the best feminism offers to women? Life, one would hope, is more than a fierce quest for self-serving independence, political power, and economic success.

If feminism is to remain relevant, it needs to start constructing a life. Feminists have done their utmost to pull the rug out from under marriage by advocating extra-marital sex as a behavioral norm (as though sex is the ultimate purpose of marriage) and by denigrating the institution of marriage in their quest to marginalize and emasculate men, as though these tactics, by themselves, supply for women an adequate emotional alternative to marriage. But the ploy is not working particularly well. Men are not really playing along with their game, and neither are many women; thankfully, there are any number of sensible men and women who are more than happy to satisfy their desires for something more collegial and hopeful than the vision feminism offers. This, ultimately, is probably why women who opt for traditional marriage and family so frustrate the feminist movement. Rather than letting women be free to choose the life that suits them best, the feminists, especially the radical wing, labor under the omnipresent leftist dilemma: the whole utopian ideal collapses unless it can force everyone else to go along.

Until the feminists realize that their movement has to acknowledge a legitimate place and role for men—and not just brow-beaten, weak, and effeminate men or gays, but strong, masculine, confident, and assertive men—feminism must be, for most people, an irrelevancy. And in that light: being a husband and father is a perfectly legitimate and worthy role for men. Having a wife and children provides men, not with the only reason, but with the *only important and good reason*, for striving to succeed. If feminists exercised more sense or imagination, they would understand that marriage, instead of being an institution designed to "keep women down," is an institution designed, among other things, to civilize all of us, to give direction and purpose to our competitive and aggressive drives, to give motivation and meaning to our striving and labor, and to provide for the very real needs of spouses and children out of love and duty, rather than begrudgingly out of charity and entitlement. There is no justification on earth to claim that marriage and family does not, or should not, bestow tremendous benefits upon both women and men, as well as their children. That feminism does not recognize this and acknowledge this and embrace this is an indication of its worthlessness to great numbers of women.

It is hard to overstate the social destruction wrought to a significant extent by the feminist movement in this one area of undermining marriage. For example, anyone who has experienced divorce, either as a child of divorced parents or as one of the parties to a divorce, is usually no stranger to the economic and emotional devastation so frequently visited upon the spouses (and children) of the men or women who abandon them for sunnier environments. But as bad as that is, it is only part of the picture. Because divorces have become so easy to obtain and become so blameless regardless of blame, marriage itself has lost much of its meaning even for those who believe in it. Young couples today can glibly recite their vows "until death do us part" with the persistent awareness, in the back of their minds, that they do not really have to intend what they say. Gone is the absolute need of affianced couples to take into consideration the very long term impacts of what marriage should entail.

Today, supermarket tabloids overflow with news of divorces and affairs and weddings and re-marriages and "blended" families, things that only 50 years ago were rather scandalous but which today are commonplace. Broadcasting the worst of these examples in public, with not a hint of condemnation or disparagement, has helped and encouraged society to accept the failure of marriage as an acceptable standard. It has cheapened and undermined the institution of marriage itself, to the point that a marriage that ends in divorce after 20 years is regarded by others as a "successful" marriage compared to the one that lasts 10 years or, worse, 10 months or 10 days.

Through the normalization of divorce, marriage has been transformed into something it never was before. Historically, marriage, as the fundamental relationship between man and woman and the foundation of the relationship between parents and children, has been a microcosm of the relationship between a benevolent government and the governed, between the Church and its flock, between God and man. In this way, it has represented a binding obligation, one that is owed not merely to an individual, but to society in general. This undertaking of duty and responsibility has been in the service of strengthening the bonds that tie all people to one another, with the implicit understanding that by meeting our obligations and by giving of oneself for the benefit of a larger whole, even in small ways, we are contributing to the overall good. Consequently, the procreation of children has historically been part and parcel of marriage; children provide continuity to all of these relationships and affirm their validity. The word "matrimony" contains the root word "mater," meaning "mother," and it is through marriage, initially, that the mother is created. Marriage establishes the foundation through which individuals take on a solemn responsibility for the welfare of others, beginning, initially, with their spouses, and then outwardly from there to children, to family, to community, and to society. Consequently, breaking the bonds of marriage is not liberation from oppression, whatever feminists may think, but liberation from obligation—a distinction that is not semantic, but fundamental.

Today, the popular concept of marriage has almost no traces left of this structure or understanding, and it is hardly surprising that almost every other social institution has broken down in consequence, with the corresponding need for "social programs" to pick up the pieces. The transformation of the institution of marriage away from the foundation of all of society into a "private" matter is a modern interpretation, and, quite frankly, has not shown itself to be particularly workable. This modern viewpoint confuses the *institution of marriage* with the *relationship of marriage*, as though the feelings of the two individuals involved are all that define the institution. But couples involved in a divorce, particularly when children are involved, quickly realize that the breakdown is not merely between themselves, but between great numbers of people: children and parents, grandchildren and grandparents, in-laws, siblings, uncles, aunts, co-workers, friends, neighbors, even schools, banks, creditors, employers, and the government. It is a fiction that marriage, *as an institution*, is just a matter between two people; marriage is a public act that involves great swaths of society.

This attempt to ignore or obscure the broad social realities of the institution of marriage by redefining it only in terms of a personal, impermanent, and self-serving enterprise is precisely why the public today is having a debate about whether gay and lesbian couples should be allowed to "marry," since, apparently, the concept of a "civil union" is not sufficiently "equal." What the feminists, the homosexual community, and everyone else who advances this idea do not realize is that "marriage," by tradition and by cultural necessity, is supposed to be more than a cozy word that connotes a status and a relationship. But because that is all marriage represents today, the feminists and their fellow-travelers are using a word, "marriage", which once was used to denote a venerable social and sacred institution, as a tool for social engineering and cultural destruction.

In the end, perhaps rather than questioning whether homosexuals should be allowed to marry, it would be more pertinent to question whether *anyone* should be "entitled" to marry, if what we are talking about is *what marriage is intended to be*. In fact, instead of expanding the reach of "marriage" to homosexual unions, the American legal regime might be better served in the quest for "equality" by extending the availability of "civil unions" to heterosexual couples, because what is often called a "marriage" today is a mere shadow of the genuine article. One might even argue that feminists, being vehemently opposed to marriage, should be the first to embrace that concept. But the reason they do not is that these social engineers are not so much interested in extending the institution of "marriage" to homosexuals, but in muscling the word "marriage" around ever more brand-new meanings—meanings that all but destroy the true meaning of marriage. It is disheartening to contemplate, but all that may ultimately transpire is that those who understand what marriage means will be forced to take the radical step of ceding the word "marriage" itself to this modern sensibility, and to coin a new name for the sacrament of marriage to reflect its historic meaning. Given the desire of these reformists to undermine the ability of religious institutions to sanctify only heterosexual unions, that may be the only recourse left once the feminists have breached this final wall, as they seem intent upon doing.

The destruction of marriage, of course, has even more far-reaching consequences for society. Since marriage is the foundation of the family and of society, the reduction of marriage to a shadow of its former self has also wrought tremendous impacts upon how our modern culture views children. In the absence of permanent marriages and fixed families, children are now viewed as optional and transient concerns, rather than as the permanent and desired continuation of a family. Modern ideas about marriage, and particularly the excesses of modern feminism, have not left children unscathed.

SECTION THREE: MOTHERHOOD

Chapter Ten: Motherhood, the *Indispensable* Female

Being a housewife is an illegitimate profession . . . The choice to serve and be protected and plan towards being a family-maker is a choice that shouldn't be. The heart of radical feminism is to change that.

--Vivian Gornick

Just what *is* the purpose of creating new life? Time and again, feminists trumpet their preoccupation with "controlling their own reproduction" at the same time they never really seem to understand why they should reproduce at all. They seem to regard motherhood as some sort of necessary evil, one more chore to add to an already full plate.

Today, people treat having of children as though it is a "lifestyle option." Children are not seen as a natural, normal, and beneficial component of a marriage and the continuation of a family . . . *let alone* a consequence of a sexual encounter . . . *let alone* necessary for human life on earth. When one really stops to think about it, modern society has become quite immature and stupid when it comes to the issue. No matter which way you cut it, sexual intercourse is how women become pregnant (at least, in the usual way), women are the ones who bear children, and children are how the world gets populated. Furthermore, bearing children is not a chore or a curse or a burden or a trial. It is simply a fact of the female sex. To women with sense and a healthy outlook on life, it is a wonderful fact.

Being the carrier and nurturer of human life is no small thing. Women who take their procreative role seriously are tremendously aware of their bodies, both with respect to the act of sex as well as their biological role in bringing forth human life and nurturing it. Any young woman interested in a future as a mother should never treat her own body with carelessness, because the care with which she treats her body can have tremendous impact not only upon her ability to conceive, but on her ability to bring a baby to term and to feed and care for it following birth.

Happily pregnant women will tell you the concerns which occupy them: the drive to ensure that they take in sufficient vitamins, the care with which they calculate the intake of sufficient quantities of folic acid, iron, protein, and fiber; the avoidance of raw or undercooked foods, of certain fish, of soft cheeses, and so on; the cravings for watermelon and ice cream (or, in my case, to everyone's disgust: liverwurst!) The responsibility is enormous: bringing another human life into this world is the ultimate responsibility of life. And the commonness of the occurrence does nothing to diminish its significance.

But many feminists seem only concerned with their bodies in a selfish way. They object most strenuously to the characterization of women as child-bearers, and disdainfully criticize more old-fashioned-minded women and men, as wanting women to be "baby factories." This is a most peculiar concept of motherhood. It sounds amazingly, and idiotically, as though they resent the fact that females bear this particular responsibility.

It requires very little reflection to realize that it is feminists who have sought to turn women into "baby factories." Rather than seeing the conception, carrying, and birth of children as normal, natural, and joyous, they focus instead upon sex, "family planning," fertility cycles, contraception, abortion, and so on, sucking every vestige of spontaneity, unexpectedness, and happiness out of the idea of new life, and injecting it with all the warmth and unpredictability of the scheduled release of next year's automobile models. Because they have embraced the idea that women not simply may, but *must*, enjoy sex solely for its self-gratifying aspects and not for its procreative promise, they have converted conception and childbirth into a rigid and cumbersome operation, one that must be approached and planned and calendared into a woman's life with efficiency and calculation. It is hard to imagine a more factory-like approach to bearing children.

What is more, the pejorative term "baby factory" is tremendously revealing about the feminist perspective on children. Not only does it, strangely and contrarily, try to characterize women who have children as something less than women, it casts babies as some sort of commodity rather than what they are: our children. The post-feminist culture has come so far from seeing the bearing and raising of children as natural and normal and *good* that America is becoming, rather unfortunately, a culture full of self-absorbed and self-serving individuals, giddy with the ability to "control" the inconveniences of nature. Utilizing these new-found tools of medical technology, feminists have helped to promote a mindset in which women may and must always put themselves first, and put their children and their husbands second (or even lower). It is as though the rejection of child-bearing is some sort of cosmic "payback" for what feminists characterize as male-dominated culture's oppression of women throughout history: men ruled the world, while the womenfolk were (we are to presume unhappily) stuck at home caring for the children that their husbands inflicted upon them (but which they would not have had if the choice had been theirs). In short, some feminists are behaving as unreasonable, petulant, and immature as the toddlers they don't want. The only problem is, what is forgivable and even endearing in a two-year-old is unattractive and absurd in grown women.

Feminism, in so many ways, attempts to subtract the role of motherhood from women, to treat it as incidental to womanhood, rather than integral. Part of this rejection likely stems from Simone de Beauvoir's *The Second Sex*, in which she explains that, as she sees it, women are defined only by reference to others—men or children—but not as humans in their own right. Modern feminism has embraced this perception wholeheartedly; consequently, it chafes at the role of motherhood because of its necessary implications of a dependent and, in many ways, subservient relationship. This concept, more than any other, is the point at which modern feminism departs from any prior concept of what it means to be a woman. While it is certainly true that a woman does not have to become a mother to be a woman, motherhood is nevertheless a *necessary* role for women; there simply are no other options. And though the mother-child relationship is clearly a dependent one, that dependency is *not* an "invention" imposed upon women by a patriarchal political order. It is, instead, simply the nature of the relationship. Modern feminism's efforts to divorce women from motherhood have done nothing to change that reality; they have simply encouraged women to behave irresponsibly.

Let's get back to the basics. It is obvious, but bears emphasis: humans are vastly unlike other animals. People do not simply bury their eggs on the beach and expect their young to come crawling out into the world on their own. Neither do humans give birth to a litter of children in the hopes that enough of them survive to keep the species going. Children are not ready to venture out and take care of themselves after a year or two. Children need attention, and they need a lot of it for a very long time. Nurturing a child to responsible and happy adulthood is a monumental task, and none is more critical. One's children are, quite literally, the future, in both a personal and a social sense; as such, the importance of raising children well surpasses every other interest a parent may have. And raising them is not a rehearsal; no parent—and no society—gets a second chance to do it right.

Children are much more than the continuation of the human species. There is another, more significant way that humans differ from other animals, and that is that humans have tremendous emotional needs. The love between a parent and child is like no other. And it is not merely incidental; it is not the love between two random people. A child is the continuation of the parents. A child should be the ultimate expression of the parents' hope and optimism for one another and for the world. There is nothing more life-affirming than to bring a child into the world; it is supposed to be a testament to courage and to love, to hope and to faith. No matter what may be happening in the world, no matter what hardships the parents face, a child represents a conviction that those issues are no cause for despair. Children help us to create an environment within our families in which we can both teach and learn the virtues of love, sacrifice, honor, devotion, selflessness, humility, and patience. With children, we can create a small oasis of peace and love within the turbulence and uncertainty of the world that surrounds us. A child must be the incarnation, quite literally, of their parents' love, and each new child should teach all of us our expanding capacity to love others, even as we reach beyond our families to our communities and to the world at large.

In this complicated world, it is not simply a matter of feeding and sheltering and clothing children and then releasing them to find their own way in the wilderness to survive or perish. Parents represent the world to their young children. From the parents, children learn what the world will hold for them, whether that is love, nurturing, and support, or indifference, neglect, and abandonment. And that lesson will be turned around and taught by that child to his or her own children, and outwardly to the rest of the world. Parenthood requires teaching children a myriad of life skills, not just in making sure they acquire knowledge with respect to practical matters, but in moral values, in personal judgment, and in physical talents. It requires providing emotional support and help in shaping attitudes, in developing analytical capabilities, and engaging in shared experiences. The list goes on and on; it is really too lengthy and too varied to catalog. The point is, parents have a responsibility to do everything they can to prepare their children not merely for life, but for a *good* life. Parents must do their utmost to help children to responsibly and capably face, more or less on their own, a very complicated and frequently threatening world at the relatively immature age of 18, although, as most parents can attest, parental responsibilities usually continue to ebb and flow well beyond that age.

This critical task is the real reason for the need to have the institutions of marriage and family robust and dominant in any culture. To this day, the family is the best social mechanism with which children can be raised. While it may be possible to find some tribe somewhere that raises children fairly successfully in a communal setting, that's the point, isn't it? Every civilization that has advanced to the point of actually providing luxuries like free time to produce an abundance of food and to seek out technological advances has done so on the basis of the nuclear family: a mother and father committed permanently to one another and to their children, and then to their extended family. Any society that failed to develop this fundamental structure has found itself unable to progress culturally, and any individual who did not have an intact family (much like today) was at a distinct disadvantage even in those societies that did progress.

Although radical feminists contend that marriage was designed to oppress women, it is evident that only someone who is extraordinarily narrow-minded could dismiss so cavalierly all of human history and almost every civilized culture throughout the world as being so single-mindedly depraved. The fact is, the intact family is essential for raising children well; no one has yet created anything remotely as successful or functional for that purpose. And, in modern times, the family is created entirely by the *voluntary* acts of the mother and father in taking that first step (no, not of having sex, but) of getting married. Women, at least, women with any sense, seek marriage before having children precisely because marriage provides the most (the *only*) reliably suitable social framework in which to raise children—that is, children who are well-provided for and happy. This is true no matter how much marriage may be claimed to impede "progress" for women. While one can wholeheartedly support and endorse marriage as an institution on its own, the reality is that marriage is less important, socially, for couples who are childless. (This is not to say that it is less important to the couple.) But once children enter the picture, that is where the marriage between the parents serves the greatest social good.

The idea that women can just as easily and successfully raise children without marriage as within it has proven to be a fallacy. Consequently, the disparagement of marriage has not achieved nothing; instead, it has succeeded in undermining the institutions that supported our society as a whole and, tragically, the institutions that to a large extent protected many women and children from the cruel demands of life: the need for financial and emotional stability and security, and the need for healthy and vigorous networks that protect them from suffering the worst effects of the inevitable ups and downs that life presents.

Providing for the needs of living has never been easy, and marriage and the family have historically provided amazingly effective safety nets for downtrodden individuals because the family operates as a unit. Through the motivation of natural affection, families foster an environment in which individuals share their resources—whether time, talent, labor, economies, or funds—that enhance the ability of every member to survive and to prosper. Lifelong marriage and the intact family were conventions that saved people, especially women and their children, from having to grasp desperately to survival in an often brutish world.

This is not to say that feminists, or anyone else for that matter, are wrong to quest for change or to want to promote causes that address the shortcomings or faults or injustices in any society. But it does mean that there is a necessary give and take; one cannot simply shove a door on one side and expect that the other side of the door is going to remain immobile. Similarly, feminists could not expect to help undermine the strength and viability of the family and think that no fallout would occur. The fact that they did, while making little or no provision for that fallout, is proof that they did not seriously reflect upon what the family represented beyond their own narrow grievances against the ills they chose to blame on marriage.

Rather than recognizing this error, today's feminist movement continues to exalt women primarily in their individual capacities, and not in ways connected to their necessary role as mothers. Too often, the maternal card is only played by feminists when it helps to achieve some political aim—for example, opposing a law by claiming it harms children in some obscure way (such as the immigration regulation opposed by NOW cited in Chapter One). But the reality is that feminism, as a movement, has been working in some measure against children from the beginning by trying too hard to extricate women from any role that requires dependence. But mothers *must be*, to varying degrees, deferential to the needs of their children. No charity or social program in the world can replace a loving and supportive mother and father, and it is quite difficult to conjecture how depending upon the capricious availability of outside help in the form of a social program presents a more "liberating" mechanism for women than a stable marriage.

Perhaps the most tragic thing about the modern feminist movement is that energy it could have dedicated in the direction of strengthening the family have instead been spent, somewhat selfishly, on helping to destroy social institutions that many women rely upon. Instead of using the new-found confidence and economic power of women to encourage better marriages and better families, it has, for the most part, moved in the opposite direction, trying to either cast these social institutions out the window or reform them so drastically that they neither bear a resemblance to the original, nor provide the same social benefits.

Unfortunately, children have too often paid the highest price for these changes.

Women continue to marry, they continue to work, and they continue to have children. If women are to succeed in marriage, career, and motherhood—in short, to succeed in the challenges that life presents—they need the tools and mechanisms in place to do so. But rather than enhance these mechanisms, the modern feminist movement—and in this, the finger must be pointed primarily at its more radical wing—has sought to destroy them. In its single-minded pursuit of an anti-marriage agenda, it has sought only to advance its own narrow interests at the expense of the other very real and very important interests women have in the well-being of their own children, not to mention themselves.

Single mothers fall into three basic categories: women who have never had a stable or (semi-) permanent relationship with the father (or fathers) of their children; women who divorce the father(s) of their children and continue to retain custody; and widowed mothers. Of all these, only in the last category might the parents be said to bear no responsibility for the plight their children may face. But the economic and social predicaments faced by women in the first two categories have been aggravated by the progressive social policies advanced by, among others, the feminist movement.

This section of the book deals with the problems created by the feminists' efforts to treat motherhood as though it is more of a biological inconvenience than a positive and beneficial social and personal commitment. First, it discusses the problems created by denying the significance of sexual responsibility for women outside of marriage without giving adequate attention to the problems—both social and personal—associated with illegitimate children. And second, it discusses the problems that have resulted from failing to promote and facilitate the stable, intact family as the norm for raising children.

Chapter Eleven: The Tragic Cost of Legitimizing Illegitimacy

The nuclear family must be destroyed, and people must find better ways of living together . . . Whatever its ultimate meaning, the break-up of families now is an objectively revolutionary process. . . . No woman should have to deny herself any opportunities because of her special responsibilities to her children . . . Families will be finally destroyed only when a revolutionary social and economic organization permits people's needs for love and security to be met in ways that do not impose divisions of labor, or any external roles, at all.

--Linda Gordon

Despite the consistent droning for the last few decades of the "reproductive control" refrain, the feminists' preferred model of industrial efficiency in childbirth is not always followed. That is, despite the widespread availability of contraception (and the perennial availability of abstinence), for large numbers of women, pregnancy is not only unplanned, but, incredibly, unanticipated. That is because there is, to a considerable degree, an inherent contradiction in expecting women to simultaneously exercise both precise preventative care and casual experimentation when it comes to engaging in sex.

Unplanned pregnancies for single women result precisely because, with alarming frequency, women *fail* to exercise control over their reproductive capacities. In fact, for all that many "modern" teenagers and unmarried young women are willing to experiment with sex, their intimate acquaintance with sexual activity is too rarely accompanied by a corresponding knowledge or appreciation of their own body's processes. As a result, pregnancy often comes about in a perfectly natural messy and chaotic way. And, also quite naturally, that has resulted in large numbers of illegitimate children—that is, children born to single young mothers who did not plan on having those children. This fact undoubtedly troubles feminists; yet, despite the size of the problem, it never occurs to them to take the obvious and sensible step of unequivocally advising young women to desist from engaging in sex unless and until they have not only learned about the potential consequences, but given sufficient thought to whether they are prepared to deal with those consequences.

On the contrary, feminism, as an ideology, is persistently tolerant of casual sexual experimentation (or even licentiousness) at the same time feminists carry on about the necessity for women to be able to "control their own reproduction," as though the question is merely one of pharmaceutical or clinic access. The carelessness with which they approach the issue of sex is precisely why they are compelled to support abortion. It is also why pharmaceutical companies have dedicated so much research to "thoughtless" contraception and "whoops, I forgot" abortifacients. There is enormous profit in female recklessness.

Today, the feminist movement is less interested in the fact that women are behaving in these self-destructive ways than in coming up with new ways for other people to rescue women from that destruction. Thus, rather than encouraging women to truly be the masters of their own fates, feminism advocates abortion, as though it offers a comprehensive solution to the plight of women who find themselves with an unwanted pregnancy. But this is woefully inadequate. Feminists can hardly advocate "choice" if what they are really arguing is that women who cannot support themselves and their children should simply abort. Abortion cannot simultaneously be both a personal right and a social duty unless one is willing to unabashedly adopt eugenics (that is, the movement to "weed out" genetically or socially undesirable people from the population). And neither is it sufficient, as NOW invariably proposes in the alternative, that the government pick up the tab for raising these children. While the government certainly could be doing more to provide assistance or incentives to single mothers, the government's job is not essentially to clean up after people's follies, or to alleviate the consequences of their poor decisions.

It is unconscionable for feminists, as the alleged champions of women's independence, *not* to address this issue as one of *actual* reproductive responsibility, rather than as a more general "social" problem. Sexual activity is neither a right nor a rite of passage, but a very serious activity suitable *only* for women who are prepared to undertake the responsibility of motherhood, both economically and psychologically. While this does not preclude educating young women and young men about contraception, the fact remains that contraception is not a "solution," it is a stopgap for what is essentially recklessness. While groups like NOW waste time blaming "abstinence only" programs for the deplorable ignorance of young people about the causes and prevention of pregnancy and sexually transmitted diseases, they are missing the more important point: young men and women simply have no concept what is at stake when engaging in sex, and generally demonstrate little interest in educating themselves. And this will remain true so long as society continues to treat the question of having sex as though it is simply a neutral and inconsequential matter of "personal choice," like whether one prefers to eat a hot dog or a hamburger.

For example, citing a controlled study on "abstinence only" programs, NOW gleefully recounts statistics demonstrating that these programs had "no impact" on whether participants engaged in sex, the age at which they began having sex, the number of partners, and the rates of pregnancy or sexually transmitted diseases. But while these statistics certainly demonstrate the failure of the "abstinence only" programs in convincing adolescents to actually abstain, they hardly prove NOW's argument that contraception education could remedy the problem: if there is no difference, there is no difference. If anything, the study made only one point worth noting: adolescents exhibit a high degree of very risky ignorance. This is not a surprise.

Feminists and other "modern" thinkers willfully mischaracterize the essential problem. They think educating young men and women about contraception can stem the increase in illegitimate children, sexually transmitted diseases, and numbers of abortions. But while education can be valuable, it does not necessarily inform the *judgment* of adolescents. As long as society treats this issue with so little gravity, teens will continue to be blissfully ignorant of what is at stake, no matter how much information they are force-fed about contraception and disease prevention, and they will carry this attitude with them into adulthood. The lackadaisical attitude that society exhibits toward adolescents (and everyone else) having indiscriminate sex, coupled with the blind (and unsubstantiated) faith that contraception education can sufficiently address the problem, is like giving helmets, coats, axes, hoses, and extinguishers to untrained individuals and sending them into a burning building. They may have the proper tools in hand and they may even know how the tools work, but they have no idea of the dangers they face or how to handle those dangers when they come to bear. Consequently, when rational thought and attention is given to the practical realities of the situation, it is abundantly clear that contraception education does precious little to address the issue of unplanned pregnancy for young women, and particularly for teenagers, because most young people simply have an atrociously inadequate appreciation for what their bodies are designed to do. Even more, contraception is inherently unreliable: not necessarily because of any failures of medical technology (although that plays a factor), but because of the lack of judgment and sense of responsibility that are simply normal attributes of immaturity.

Again, it should strike anyone with common sense that it is ludicrous to argue that many adolescents lack the necessary self-control to restrain their sexual urges, yet will nevertheless retain the presence of mind to be assiduously careful about birth control. The bottom line that needs to be faced is that fertile women who have sex with moderate frequency are quite likely to become pregnant. Nature has a funny way of being persistent, particularly when trying to detour around one's biological functions are cumbersome and unpleasant. And this is not merely an admonition for 15- and 16- year-olds who, in any case, should not be expected, much less encouraged, to exercise good judgment about such important decisions as whether—and with whom—to engage in sex. (And nearly everyone will acknowledge that *these are* important decisions.) The unfortunate but stark reality is that 20- to 30-year old men and women hardly exhibit better self-discipline or intelligence.

It defies sense for feminists to take the position that, on the one hand, young women are too ignorant or undisciplined to fully appreciate the fact that self-control may spell the difference between achieving their ambitions and facing hardship in life, yet, on the other hand, retain the intellectual capacity to understand how to employ their budding sexuality. Several decades of an unremitting increase in the number of unwed mothers, coupled with the corresponding and severe decline in the well-being of those single mothers and their children, offer compelling evidence that the sexual revolution has fallen far short of its promises of sexual "freedom" for women, the Pill, abortion, and condoms notwithstanding. This is not to say that there are not responsible (or fortunate) young women who have successfully navigated the sexual minefield. But when it comes to sexual activity, the evidence is abundantly clear that the "choice" young women face is not simply between "having sex" and "not having sex", but may more aptly be characterized as between "fear, worry, anguish, STDs, pregnancy, abortion, abandonment, and unwed motherhood" and "not having sex."

What kind of feminist movement is it that refuses to tell young women to stand up for themselves, to accept full responsibility for the decisions they make, and to take charge of their own lives? At some point, to substantiate the claim that it cares about the mental, physical, and economic welfare of young women, it is necessary for feminism to point out that "reproductive responsibility" requires just that: a conscious exercise of informed and prudent decision-making and self-discipline, including knowing when to avoid those risks that one would rather not gamble upon.

Promoting the idea of sexual prudence and restraint as a social norm will not prevent all irresponsible sexual activity, but there is no reason to believe that advancing that message will have *no* influence on young women, particularly if it comes from feminist quarters. A message of taking sex seriously is just as likely to impact young women as much as the opposite message of casual sexual experimentation has had on the young men and women to whom it has been preached for at least four decades. And while feminism universally rejects ideas of religion-based morality, there are any number of non-religious ethical arguments in favor of sexual responsibility that should be compelling enough. If the facts of economics and the acknowledged difficult experiences of single mothers fail to persuade, it should strike anyone as strange, to say the least, that the same young women who are sensitive to the ethics involved in the use of, for example, Genetically Modified Organisms in the food they eat today, seem to think nothing of consuming a steady diet of synthetic hormones or other drugs directly into their own bodies, and further expelling them as waste, where the effects of such synthetic hormones are having dramatic effects on the environment. If nothing else, young women might stop to consider the wisdom of entrusting their future health to the benevolence and reliability of the pharmaceutical industry and the medical profession.

Young women should be taught the importance of accepting individual responsibility with respect to the predictable and normal consequences of their behavior. With a few exceptions, many women who put themselves in untenable situations with respect to becoming single mothers are not simply *victims*, they are *culprits* in their own demise. While one can readily support the idea that single mothers should not be treated as social outcasts, it is hypocritical for the women's movement to argue that women are entitled to respect unless it also supports the idea that accountability does, in fact, matter. Victimhood is not very useful for conferring self-esteem; victimhood does not foster in young women a self-image of strength and confidence.

True, one can reasonably argue that wayward men are just as much to blame for their corresponding irresponsibility of begetting illegitimate children, but it is unrealistic for feminists to rely too much on that bandwagon. Nothing can change the fact that women are the ones who have to shoulder (or, more aptly, stomach) the load of unplanned pregnancy and its outcome of unprovided-for children. Not only does the argument about male irresponsibility prove nothing, it is rather like legislating against facial hair: we may all be subject to the law, but only men will have to shave.

Moreover, it is contradictory to argue, as many feminists do, that men should step in to assume responsibility for the unplanned pregnancies of unmarried women if those same women have demonstrated too little interest in being responsible for themselves. Women, as a group, cannot claim to be capable of making decisions for themselves if, in the end, they ultimately want men to bear the responsibility of the decisions they make. More, feminists cannot blast men as "oppressive" for wanting to protect women, yet demand that men nevertheless step in to protect women from the worst consequences of their own unwise behavior. If exclusive and unilateral "reproductive control" of their bodies is what feminists are demanding for women, then women must demonstrate that they have the capacity to exercise it. This may sound like a harsh judgment, and, truly, it is—and it is even patently unfair. But the reality is exactly that harsh: chasing down errant fathers for child support is, for the most part, not really solving problems for women who bear children outside of marriage. As unjust as it may be, it is *young women, not young men,* who need to understand the gravity of what it means to engage in loose sexual activity.

The results of taking the contrary and "tolerant" view of sex have been utterly disastrous and predictable: women are having children all the time—they are just too often having them outside of marriage. While this has been happening in some small measure throughout history, there is no getting around the fact that feminism has sought not only to remove any taboo from this behavior, they have sought to normalize it and, to some extent, institutionalize it. Quite expectedly, out of wedlock childbirth is therefore becoming not only common, but, today, almost prevalent, particularly among minority and poor communities. As a rule, this has been detrimental for the women who attempt it and, even more unfortunately, detrimental to their children and to society. This has been documented time and again, and it is futile to dispute the evidence as saying anything other than what it says.

While one need not rehash all the alarming statistics here, some pertinent information bears repeating. A mother who bears and raises children outside of marriage is roughly seven times more likely to live in poverty than a woman who has children within a marriage. Further, as Maggie Gallagher heartbreakingly pointed out in her study *The Abolition of Marriage*, raising a child without the presence of a father leaves a significant emotional need unfulfilled in children, no matter how much sociologists and psychologists play it down; and exceptions to this rule are hardly proof against the norm. While individual children certainly can cope without fathers, coping is not the same as thriving. And, when fatherlessness is repeated throughout a community, it is one of most predictive factors of crime and other severely antisocial behavior—more predictive, in fact, than simple poverty. Thus, feminists, who like to make a virtue of the fact that women do not need husbands, too easily ignore the reality that their children, however, most often need fathers.

But the damage of normalizing single motherhood does not end with crime and social costs. It has tremendous personal costs on mothers and children. The simple fact is, raising a child takes both time and resources. Consequently, the problem is hardly worth analysis: given that the vast majority of people trade their time for money—that is, they work for a living—something has to give when it comes to child-raising department. It is elementary that two-parent families can better cope with the time and money trade-offs required to raise children.

Even if one were to accept, as a given, that the world *ought to be* the way the feminists want, that is, that the taxpayers through the government should happily and generously dole out enough health, housing, and food benefits to single mothers so that they and their children can live in comfort and without worries, the fact remains that *that world does not exist*. And because it does not exist, it is deplorable that the feminist movement does not educate women on *what the world really does offer*—and that means educate, not whine, complain, and rant. That real world is almost unremittingly harsh to never-married single mothers. And hoping for a different world tomorrow does little to empower women today.

The only hope for some single mothers today *is* a social program, although simple welfare is demonstrating its inadequacy in supplying the answer. Never married mothers, and more importantly, their children, do not need mere survival; they need a viable and permanent road out of their predicament. The unfortunate reality is that, in our society today, unmarried mothers plainly cannot depend upon entering into a stable family relationship as an avenue for escaping, or at least defending against, persistent economic pressures. If anything, such mothers likely need a network of volunteer help, self-help, and, most importantly, cooperative help. In short, they need social structures that approximate the benefits of family, resources that can provide their children with the care and attention they need while these mothers bolster their ability to support themselves and their children to the point where truly liberating opportunities become available to them. They need a system in place that can break them of dependence on the subsistence or welfare that is likely to bind them and their children into permanent poverty and social devastation.

While NOW acknowledges this need, one is hard-pressed to find any feminist-inspired movement that has undertaken to materially help women in this situation by founding, funding, and operating organizations for women that offer the kind of support that an intact family might have provided. The reality is that feminism, true to its leftist politics, consistently allocates the responsibility for remedying these social "injustices" onto someone—anyone—but the people actually responsible. It then tells women that their hardships are the fault of unsympathetic or sexist male legislators who have failed to provide them adequate safety nets, as though that provides any material help, let alone consolation. In contrast, groups that work in opposition to the stated goals of the feminist movement (even if not overtly) seem to be the ones to step in to help women deal with their very real problems: private or faith-based community charities.

Too often, feminists get away with disowning any blame for some of the social problems they have abetted or facilitated. But less important than any culpability feminism may have in its causation is that it is doing little to work against its perpetuation, no matter how many women it continues to affect. There is no question that the feminist movement embraced and advocated the sexual revolution as part and parcel of its platform of liberation, and it continually puts the lion's share of its considerable weight behind "reproductive control," as though the Pill and *Roe v. Wade* together constitute an easily playable "get out of motherhood free" card. Yet the evidence is clear that, as a means of guaranteeing liberation for great numbers of young women, these mechanisms have proven to be grossly inadequate.

In failing to take a responsible stand, feminism essentially preys upon impoverished single mothers, and offers them up as a sacrifice in pursuit of its agenda. Standing by as this catastrophe unfolds mirrors exactly the leftist strategy of encouraging and abetting disaster in order to force into existence the social changes they desire. Feminism, as a political force, wholeheartedly employs this methodology in willingly consigning scores of immature and overburdened young women to the slate of casualties for our cultural failings, then channeling these young women into a life that is utterly dependent upon and beholden to its leftist ideology. This strategy is based almost entirely upon the falsehood, touted by feminism, that contraception and abortion can easily and painlessly protect women from having to control their own weaknesses.

By helping to minimize the critical importance of marriage in the motherhood equation, feminism, as a movement, is now working at the fringes of the issues that concern the many women for whom feminism once held promise. Instead of confronting and conquering new frontiers for women, the movement is now preoccupied with addressing the worst consequences of the social problems and public policy disasters that it helped to advance. These causes, such as supporting a healthcare program for impoverished single mothers and their children, may need a champion (unfortunately), and they may all be near and dear to feminists, but they are part of an agenda that attempts to fix what has failed, not an agenda that promotes success, and there is a world of difference. Throwing a drowning woman a life preserver after you have tossed her in the sea may be helpful, but she would have been better served if you had, instead, begun the process by teaching her how to swim. By simply asserting, without any evidence to support it, that women could have sex without consequence, and that they could and ought to successfully manage motherhood on their own, the feminist movement, unfortunately, employed the former tactic.

As noted above, while feminism is certainly not the only culprit in the demise of the family, its influence has been significant. To a certain extent, feminism's denial of any culpability on this issue is based upon misunderstanding how its message has been translated into the culture. For the most part, feminism's social philosophies have always been aimed at the upper economic spheres, at fairly well-off educated young women who encounter its more radical ideas on college campuses. In that sphere, feminist theories supply only a thin veneer of pretension that cannot overcome two decades of middle-class upbringing. Thus, the same young women who might rant about the injustices of the institution of marriage among their college companions will, just a few years later, ecstatically plan their own full-blown church wedding, white dress and all.

Consequently, feminism becomes merely a stylish intellectual outfit. Many women, relatively affluent and well-educated, feel liberated enough to promote ideas like sexual freedom because they can discount how that translates into reality by the persistent undercurrent of their actual position: *"Other* women must have the freedom to behave as they wish, even if *I* find it disagreeable or exercise sufficient self-discipline, or *I* have the resources and support to avoid negative consequences." This is also the heart of the liberal's moral evasion on issues like abortion: "personally, I am against it, but I cannot tell other women what to do." Sexual irresponsibility is easy to promote or tolerate when it remains an intellectual exercise and placed under the universally appealing banner of "freedom," but not when it is correctly characterized as "irresponsibility" with a harsh and unforgiving reality. By demanding that government fund contraception and abortion services, feminists pretend that sexual permissiveness is not the costly indulgence that it is, but an entitlement—never mind its sordid results.

Feminism's ideas about sexual freedom and having children outside of marriage have gained purchase throughout the last four decades, and their consequences now manifest themselves in depressing and tragic ways. They have taken root in and disrupted those older tempering influences, such that even upper- and middle-class women are finding themselves facing the economic and social difficulties that accompany unwed motherhood. And, as mentioned previously, these ideas have especially gained a strengthened foothold in the lower economic strata, where teen pregnancy, illegitimacy, fatherlessness, welfare, and crime are more common, and thus there is significantly less stigma attached to them. These "progressive" ideas, now becoming dominant in the culture, have been enormously destructive to the welfare of society overall.

Feminists and their fellow-travelers in this progressive revolution are engaged in social experimentation; there is no other way to characterize it. The ideas they have endorsed—discarding marriage and the traditional family as the norm for routine sexual activity, and its necessary consequence of bearing and raising children outside of a nuclear family—have never been tried before as a pervasive practice; moreover, they have consistently failed even at the outer fringes of mainstream society. They are like the teacher who decides to try a new method of teaching math: when an entire class fails the standardized math exam, she throws up her hands and says, "I guess that way doesn't work." The only problem, of course, is that an entire class of children now has no idea how to do math. It is not enough to conclude, "Oh, well, back to the drawing board," or to say that math is not very important, anyway, or claim, without any evidence whatsoever, that the children are better off not knowing math. And so one must ask: how can a legitimate feminist movement so blithely cast off a whole subpopulation of women as helpless and futureless?

The women who succumbed to the feminist mindset in regard to sex and children outside of marriage are not, as a group, better off now than before the women's movement embarked on this experiment. Trading one set of problems for another set is hardly progress. It can hardly be called a victory for liberation if women have been freed from the "patriarchal slavery" induced by the formerly dominant social institution of marriage only to be subject to the less forgiving master of perpetual poverty. At some point, even feminists must have realized that the history of marriage has a slightly more nuanced significance beyond an unrelenting endeavor to subjugate women.

Having and raising children is a critical responsibility, not merely in a personal sense for parents, but very much in a social context. And it is one which women *must* bear, whether feminists like that fact or not. Reality is *not* optional. The women now struggling at the lower rungs of society attempting to raise children on their own without any semblance of a marriage or family may not be feminists, but to a large degree they are the product of feminist (and other) efforts to undermine and deconstruct family structure as the norm for rearing children. It is true one cannot discount the personal responsibility of these young women who succumbed to the modern ethos. But it becomes more difficult to entirely blame them when they are being told, consistently and vehemently, that women are simply "victims," and not active participants in their own lives. With its message of "progressive" reform, society conspires to deliberately conceal from young women the reality that the decisions they may make about sex while in the throes of immature and ignorant adolescence are very serious indeed, and are likely to have tremendous bearing on their long-term fates. Even a cursory survey of social demographics demonstrates, as a general and incontrovertible rule, that the women who are succeeding—*even as feminists*—have done so more often by rejecting the modern ethos in favor of adhering more closely to traditional mores when it comes to bearing and raising children. If today's impoverished single mothers had sought stable marriages as a prerequisite to having children, they might now have truly achieved some measure of independence and liberation.

It may seem too easy to lay this problem at the feet of the feminist movement, but it has been—*has promoted itself as*—a leader in the culture wars to redefine how women ought to behave and what responsibilities women should bear. And the reality is that feminists have endorsed a vision of womanhood that is in fundamental ways irresponsible, both with respect to sexual behavior and to the rearing of children. Furthermore, for them to pass this problem off to the government or to anyone else is to undermine the very thing they supposedly stand for: empowerment and independence. It hardly helps to elevate the status of women, generally, if feminism's universal response to women facing hardships is to tell them—and, significantly, to tell the rest of the world—that women are passive, ignorant victims who need to be saved by the government.

This is a stark and clear example of how feminism is failing women, notwithstanding all of its nice-sounding rationales. The fact is, advocating marriage as a precursor to motherhood as a social norm and as a social good is not simply a political position, *it has proven itself to be an economic and pragmatic necessity.* By discarding marriage and embracing single motherhood in the complete absence of any social system that was designed to support it, feminism put the cart before the horse. By refusing to take a responsible position, it continues to demonstrate its willingness to sacrifice women in pursuit of its leftist agenda, all under the deceptive guise of claiming to "help" women.

Clearly, successful single motherhood is no small achievement, and it is appropriate to laud the women who achieve it. But as a rule, single motherhood is hardly a recipe for independence or economic stability, and it is not an ideal way in which to raise children, even for those mothers who, against all odds, and in the face of tremendous self-sacrifice, succeed.

Chapter Twelve: The Children of Divorce in the Age of "Equality"

The end of the institution of marriage is a necessary condition for the liberation of women. Therefore it is important for us to encourage women to leave their husbands and not to live individually with men.

--Declaration of Feminism 1971

The other half of the fatherless problem in our nation is that caused by divorce. And unfortunately, divorced mothers, particularly those of young children and multiple children, are sometimes not in a substantially better financial condition than single mothers who never married. Why is this a feminist issue? Because in denigrating marriage, the feminists have offered divorce as a simple, welcome, and easily accessible "remedy" for unsatisfactory marriages, even when children are involved. Further, they have encouraged the idea that divorced mothers can and should fend for themselves economically just as easily as divorced fathers, even when women retain custody of their children.

Divorce has become commonplace, and divorce laws have followed the feminist pattern: men and women are treated "equally" by the law, regardless of the economic realities that governed the marriage while it was intact. But how has divorce affected mothers? The economic consequences of divorce on mothers was the subject of the book *The Equality Trap* by Mary Ann Mason. The thesis of Ms. Mason's book is straightforward. Basically, she pointed out that the notion of "equality" is fine so long as men and women are truly equal: single, well-educated and trained, and unencumbered by the responsibilities of parenthood. Thus, the feminist's push to equalize the treatment of men and women by the law does not necessarily have adverse economic consequences on childless women.

But even there, changes in divorce laws that equalized divisions of assets and economic burdens have the nasty aspect of changing the terms of an already existing agreement: women who had never had a career, or who suspended their careers, or who decided to forego advancement in their careers in favor of relying upon their husband's income during the marriage, often come to find themselves, after divorce, left with a share of the assets and severely limited career prospects. This has been particularly devastating to older women who are both more likely to have been of an old-school, traditional wifely mindset (and thus with little work experience), as well as to be less attractive to employers: why hire an older woman with little experience, when a much younger woman with the same experience will be around to contribute when her skill-set becomes valuable?

Even in community property states, where the division of marital assets is "equal" no matter who provided the income that purchased those assets, women frequently come out worse, because the earning potential of each spouse is often greatly skewed. Asset division in divorce laws frequently resorts to the fiction that married individuals can simply pretend as though the marriage never occurred. It sounds nice in theory, but it is completely unrealistic. Saying, "Okay, that's that. You're on your own now!" completely ignores the fact that that was not the deal that was struck when the marriage was made. Even standard contract law recognizes that one party to a contract cannot simply violate the contract and then just walk away scot free. Under normal contract law, a party that lives up to his part of a deal is entitled to the benefit of the deal—and does not merely get his money back.

But the real downside of the "equality" illusion in divorce occurs when there are children involved. There is simply no possible way for a single parent, male or female, to compete on a level playing field with individuals who do not have children or with married individuals (childless or not). As Ms. Mason's book so clearly points out (and which feminists will readily concede), mothers often end up as the primary caretakers of children, especially very young children, and most single-parent households are households headed by women. Once you appreciate that fact, the idea that women can somehow dedicate themselves to their careers with the same zeal as a single man or single woman is simply nonsense, except, perhaps, in those rarified instances where the level of compensation allows for the hiring of nannies or *au pairs*, or where the children have reached an age where little supervision is required (even if it may be desirable!). But few women have the financial resources of Madonna before embarking upon motherhood.

As a result, single mothers, regardless of their education or qualifications, are frequently at a distinct disadvantage in the marketplace. The greatest female lawyer in the world is unlikely to become a partner at a large firm if she has to leave the office before 6:00 p.m. to pick up her children before the close of the day-care facility, or if she is unable to work on weekends for lack of a babysitter. And, of course, the reality is that many divorced mothers have nowhere near the earning capacity of a lawyer: most men and women have more pedestrian skills available to the job market. Without the help of a husband and father, parenthood coupled with the burden of having to earn a decent living is quite simply a monumental responsibility to shoulder for a single mother. This is especially so when you consider the additional resources that children consume, not only in the way of easily measurable factors like food, clothing, (larger) housing, and the income-offsetting expense of daycare, but in the additional cost of often-overlooked indirect needs, such as the desire to live in a safe neighborhood, to live in a house that lies within reasonable distance of a decent school, and so on.

But feminists rarely give sufficient weight to this concern, at least in the context of discouraging divorce as an "answer." For example, NOW generally pays attention to the divorce picture *only* in the context of abusive situations, where it is easy to justify divorce as the best option for women and their children. This sort of tunnel vision too readily ignores the needs of most of the children who become embroiled in a divorce—and, incidentally, the needs of the mothers who care for them. Ignoring and downplaying the impacts of the casual divorce culture has had terrible consequences for many single mothers, such that, even with child-support, financially, fathers can anticipate that they will be substantially better off in the aftermath of divorce, and mothers with primary custody can expect to be substantially worse off, particularly if very young children are involved. In the absence of any blame or responsibility in the divorce equation, men can frequently walk away from their paternal obligations with a light heart and a heavy wallet. And it is not uncommon, unfortunately, for those fathers to disappear entirely from their children's lives emotionally, and to cut off their children from support the minute they hit their eighteenth birthdays. This, in turn has left many single mothers with the burden of trying to fund their children's college educations on their own in the hope that, with it, their children will be able to succeed in life while they struggle to put something—anything—aside for their own retirement.

Certainly, one cannot excuse men from shirking their parental responsibilities. But that knowledge is cold comfort for the bitter reality. The mothers caught in the divorce trap who turn their anger towards their ex-husbands and, occasionally, toward men in general, rarely question why the bright future they envisioned on their wedding day has degenerated into a struggle for existence.

At one time, divorce courts viewed children as the primary focus of their concerns, and quite readily chastised parents for sacrificing the best interests of their children in favor of the interests served by their own (in comparison) sometimes petty wrangling. And when divorces were granted—for specific reasons—courts frequently saw to it that children were provided for, regardless of the impact on either parent. But in the modern divorce mindset, supported by modern divorce laws, a deserting or irresponsible spouse is not forced to feel the slightest twinge of responsibility or culpability in the emotional, and often financial, train wreck to which they are subjecting their spouse and children.

Frequently, one hears the argument that children are "better off" by a divorce, because they are spared their parents incessant arguments or disaffection. And certainly, in cases of abuse or other serious and irresolvable or intolerable circumstances, the interests of the children may be better served by the dissolution of a marriage. But that is a small portion of today's divorces. Too often, divorces occur simply because of a sort of laziness and cowardice: the refusal to put effort into the marriage by either party because it no longer suits their tastes, because they are tired of shouldering their responsibilities, and because they prefer to think only of their own desires rather than the needs of others. The relative ease of just not trying, or the novelty of directing one's energies in a new direction or toward a new partner, are simply too seductive when divorce is so easy to obtain. In such cases, sparing the children from verbal battles is simply an excuse for a parent to do what he or she wants to do in the first place, and it addresses only one aspect of the divorce picture. It ignores the alternative hardships and emotional damage to which the children are quite often subjected following divorce, such as a neglectful or alienated parent, a revolving door of parental substitutes, being replaced in their parent's affection by new spouses, new half-siblings or new step-siblings, the feelings of betrayal by their parents, and so on.

Moreover, the argument that children are "better off" only operates when parents are indulged in the belief that their interests are more important than their children's. Just as one commits to a spouse in marriage, fathers and mothers need to understand and accept that once they commit to children—simply by virtue of having them—they no longer have the ability to do what they selfishly please. Until our society returns to the conviction that responsibility for one's children is not simply an "option" or, worse, merely an economic arrangement, children of divorce will forever be sacrificed on the altar of their parents' interests. Divorce has been refashioned into an assertion only of rights and interests, but rarely is marriage and parenthood considered to be a more forceful counterweight of shouldering responsibilities and obligations.

To a certain degree, the feminist movement is able to take advantage of the problems created by the vicious circumstance of modern divorce. Feminists have exalted the single working mother as more heroic than the married, stay-at-home mother. And although NOW, unlike the radical feminists, does not denigrate stay-at-home mothers, it tends to ignore or overlook the critical importance of marriage itself in meeting the challenges that motherhood presents. Divorced mothers dealing with the troubles inherent in their situation often end up feeling victimized, and sympathetic to the idea that their troubles can be blamed upon society and upon men. While NOW provides useful resource information for divorced and divorcing mothers, it does not flatly acknowledge that the troubles of raising children on one's own are not primarily the result of victimization, but of pragmatic realities: having two parents at home eases the burdens inherent in raising children by allowing those burdens to be shared.

With divorce, men have too often been handed the ticket to their moral as well as financial freedom, despite the weight of responsibilities that should have governed their behavior, and divorced custodial mothers have few places to turn for recourse. Years ago, a divorced working man with a non-working ex-wife and children to support could not even think of remarrying because the financial burden of supporting two families was unmanageable. Today, a divorced man often buys himself a new Corvette and dates twenty-somethings, and his divorced wife goes out looking for a better job (or simply *a* job) and a tolerably reliable and safe day-care facility. As a result, feminists can easily paint men with the broad brush of being irresponsible, callous, and selfish, and hold struggling single mothers up as the victims of masculine malevolence. But this simplified picture is not truly indicative of what has happened. Modern divorce is no longer treated by society as an admission of failure, but simply as a form of release, as though it were a pardon. As new social norms have erased any stigma of divorce and removed the financial burden of support from the breadwinner of the marital relationship, divorce becomes simply one item in a menu of lifestyle options, and not what it really is: the destruction of a family.

One should readily and deservedly praise the efforts of feminist organizations that provide help and information to women escaping abusive situations within marriage. But they are studiously noncommittal when it comes to other divorces. They stand idly by while the emotional devastation to children inflicted by their divorcing or divorced parents plays itself out. Feminists have not shown much interest at all in strengthening and supporting the intact family, in discouraging divorce or making them more difficult to obtain where abuse is absent and when children are involved. In a way, it is a sad statement, and manifestly defeatist, that organizations like NOW focus so much attention on how to deal with failure (for example, by showing women how to fight for custody and/or obtain adequate child support) rather than guide men and women toward success in this most critical social issue.

A strong marriage and family provide children with emotional, economic, and social stability. The reason the institutions of marriage and family exist, and the reasons social mores and rules were created, were not to "keep women in their place," but rather because these conventions served to form a socially cohesive whole that "worked." Moreover, it was just as limiting to men as it ever was to women. But notwithstanding all that "oppression" of men and women, these social institutions enabled people not only to merely survive, but to prosper, and to advance. In fact, they advanced to the point that women could gripe about being stuck at home with too much education and too little to do. And while one can certainly acknowledge that not every marriage is perfect, and not every family is giving and wonderful, the ones that aren't are hardly proof of the failure of marriage and family, and the proportion of failing families is not what defines whether families work. Moreover, even the failures that occur within a family are often not much worse than the alternative of being left only with the remnants of a destroyed family.

As noted previously, there are, of course, single divorced mothers who have succeeded against the weight of the odds, by raising children who are perfectly good and normal and well-adjusted, even if their husbands/fathers were far from exemplary. But holding such women up as examples, as the achievement of the feminist dream, is hardly a boon to women overall. Overcoming hardships is admirable, but it is not a norm we should try to impose or to encourage women to emulate. The fact that the rewards of motherhood *can* be achieved in this way is no reason to propose that they *should* be achieved in this way. Indeed, holding up such women as the standard simply reinforces the notion that women who are not measuring up to this extraordinary accomplishment are somehow failing, when the reality is that simply coping under these circumstances is a considerable achievement. But "coping" is not what women, as a group, should be striving for.

For the vast majority of mothers, having the positive daily presence of a husband and father should be the aim for a number of reasons, and the feminist movement should be reinforcing that undeniable fact, not discounting it or ignoring it. Good fathers not only provide a necessary role model of manhood for their sons and daughters, but they also provide the balance and support that mothers need—especially *working* mothers—given today's unprecedented demands upon their time, energy, patience, and resources. It is, in a way, unforgiveable that the feminist movement has sought to encourage women to step out of the house and into the workforce at the same time that it has encouraged society to reject marriage, as though raising children is a task that should or even can be accomplished in a woman's spare time. The fact that feminism pursues these contradictory positions demonstrates a serious disregard of the vital importance of raising children well.

There is no question that most mothers today would be best served by a women's movement that was taking affirmative steps to strengthen the family, to do what it can to make it better not only for women, but for men and children as well. As it is, the failure of feminism to openly and strongly embrace the family as the ideal social institution for raising children is subtly undermining the well-being of the many women who are wives and mothers.

SECTION FOUR: WORKING MOTHERS

Chapter Thirteen: Why Must Working Mothers Pretend Their Children Don't Matter?

At work, you think of the children you have left at home. At home, you think of the work you've left unfinished. Such a struggle is unleashed within yourself. Your heart is rent.

-- Golda Meir

If you bungle raising your children, I don't think whatever else you do well matters very much.

--Jacqueline Kennedy Onassis

As elaborated upon above, one way in which modern feminism is failing women is by condoning the idea that women either can or should easily raise children without a husband and father to help, to support them, and to provide balance and additional security for their own and their family's overall well-being. But the second way is by encouraging the perception that children may be relegated to a minor concern of working women, rather than a primary concern. In this, they have greatly disserved working mothers. The competing interests that concern women between the demands of a career and the demands of motherhood is one of the most troubling issues facing working mothers today, whether or not they are married.

This section discusses the practical difficulties confronted by mothers who have given up some child-raising responsibilities in favor of dedicating time and effort to their careers, and how little the feminist movement is doing to support them despite, and sometimes because of, its uncompromising stance on the desirability of women working outside the home, even when they have infants and toddlers. When feminists established the legal milestone of "equal" treatment in the workplace, they acted as though that achievement, all by itself, would somehow erase or equalize the roles carried out by men and women both economically and domestically. They ignored too readily the special demands of motherhood. With regard to this issue, women would have been better served if the feminist movement had fought specifically for women's rights, rather than equal rights.

To be clear: one cannot reasonably condemn mothers who work. Heaven knows, there are many reasons women and their families choose this route, not the least of which are the economic demands placed upon the modern American family today. Contrary to what many people may believe, the number of women in the American workforce today is not due simply to equal opportunity. As alluded to in NOW's 1966 Statement of Purpose, the American economy has shifted in the last half century away from requiring relatively high-paying physical labor in the manufacturing sector to needing more lower-paying office-related help in the service sector. Women have been able to fill much of the American economy's requirements for an educated but deskbound workforce. As a result, women today are a permanent fixture in the American economy. However, the relatively lower pay in the American workforce overall translates, in many cases, into the requirement that many couples must rely upon two incomes if their families want to live as well as or better than families of their parents' generation. In addition, there are practical reasons for women to bolster their financial stability and independence given the uncertainties of life; as discussed previously, divorces are now extremely easy to obtain for a disgruntled spouse, and life can always take an unexpected turn. Finally, there are personal reasons that can motivate women to succeed in business.

Notwithstanding these facts of economic life, most working women, once they become mothers, reconsider their commitment to a full-time career. This may happen no matter how much women like and feel challenged by their careers, and no matter how much they may have planned and arranged to return to work once their first child or subsequent children are born. Some women reassess their plans to the point that they decide to forego their careers entirely—at least for the time being—in favor of staying at home and dedicating their time and their talents to their families. Women who can manage to do this consider themselves fortunate to have the luxury of being able to do so. At the same time, there are other women who purposefully choose to stay at home either from the get-go or after some years dedicated to a career, but who decide after a while that they need additional outlets for their creativity and intellectual talents.

It is the attempt by women in both camps— the ones who continue working but want to spend more time at home, and the ones who stay at home but want to work in some capacity—to find a happy balance that has created a dilemma. The structure of American companies, unfortunately, too rarely provides women with opportunities to advance the interests of both family and career with anything approaching equal ardor. This has led, in some instances, to the creation of a sort of cottage industry in "mom-based" businesses and professional pursuits that allow women to allocate their time in a way that more accurately reflects the demands placed on their lives by their families, by the economy, and according to their personal priorities. For many women, that is the only valid option they have if they want to successfully juggle their obligations along with their ambitions.

Amid all this: where do the hard-line feminists stand? How have they worked to provide practical solutions that give real women viable options that allow them to design life on their own terms? Unfortunately, very little. The universal feminist response to these problems seems to be, primarily, to propose yet more government programs or mandates, such as government provided day-care or mandatory leave laws. But many women, successful women included, do not need another social program. What they need is private accommodation.

Back in 1989, Felice N. Schwartz wrote an article for the Harvard Business Review in which she proposed that American businesses should take a hard look at this issue. Schwartz pointed out two critical facts: first, women, as a general rule, provide a highly educated and productive workforce; and second, most women have children. Given the then-current (and currently predominant) structure of American businesses, she pointed out that, as a practical matter, this forced women to choose between the competing demands of career and family, and, consequently, either or both interests were bound to suffer.

What Ms. Schwartz proposed was that businesses might be wise to review this workforce demographic and formally adopt a middle ground: allow women with children the opportunity to job-share with other women or to otherwise take a lightened load, so that, instead of making an exclusive choice, they can pursue both their career interests as well as spend more time with their families, particularly when their children are very young. And while she recognized that women who opted for these positions would be temporarily side-lined in terms of career advancement, she resolved this by suggesting that women in these positions should not be viewed by their employers with prejudice, but should be able to retain their rank (rather than move downward), then have the opportunity to resume a more upward-looking career path when their family commitments allowed a full-time career. Ms. Schwartz felt that this was a reasonable resolution: it allowed working mothers who remained dedicated to their careers an opportunity to employ their talents and meaningfully contribute to their employers at the same time they did not have to completely sacrifice their obligations to their families.

Backed up by her well-laid out explanation of workforce demographics and the needs of modern business, Ms. Schwarz's proposal seemed eminently sensible. But apparently not to feminists. The response was swift and universally negative from that quarter. Almost immediately, the term "mommy-tracking" was coined—and derided as detrimental to the cause of women. In the feminist dogma, Ms. Schwartz had committed the heresy of suggesting that women wanted to be anything different—or, to the feminist mindset, *less*—than their male counterparts in the workforce. The feminists claimed that Ms. Schwartz's idea, just by its utterance, opened the door for American business to once again discriminate against women.

Notwithstanding these criticisms, however, Felice Schwartz hit the nail on the head for many mothers. Unfortunately, too few of them stepped forward to defend her idea, perhaps sensitive to the fact that, in 1989, the place of women in the American workforce did not seem so firmly established. But, strangely enough, twenty years later, many women are finally getting it. Women are also recognizing what the feminists ironically lacked the confidence to believe back in 1989 when Ms. Schwartz proclaimed it: women are too valuable to the American workforce for employers to simply write them off. Many effective and intelligent women are finding out that, when they want to leave their employers to spend time with their families, their employers are scrambling to find a way to retain them in some capacity. And rather than being discriminated against, women have sometimes found that the opposite is true: their employers would *like to* accommodate them. For example, when Pepsi-Cola North America CEO Brenda Barnes decided to resign in order to spend time with her family, Pepsi tried to retain her in some capacity by offering a more flexible schedule or an extended leave of absence. But after years of 70 hour workweeks with very little time to spend with her husband and children, she had simply had enough. What Felice Schwartz understood is that companies would be wiser to offer a solution for mothers *before* they experience the burnout that comes from stretching one's life too thin to be able enjoy both family and career.

In their striving to achieve equal treatment of men and women, the feminists purposefully and stubbornly rejected the idea that any women—including mothers—might not want to be treated the same as their male counterparts in the workforce. As a result, today, roadblocks often exist that prevent employers from treating women and men differently, even when those differences would benefit working mothers. So while some employers have allowed women to bring their babies to work, or have redefined jobs to allow women to work as "independent contractors" on their own schedule, they are exceptions to the rule, and the accommodations are frequently riddled with potential difficulties when it comes to employment law. It is often small employers who have the most flexibility, unhampered as they are by the need to rigidly apply standard rules and policies across significant populations of employees. For large employers, any policy that smacks of favoritism is an invitation to liability, and, ironically, they may offer fewer options to accommodate working mothers. Women who have wanted (or *needed*) to continue working but have a strong interest in raising their own children have had to resort to part-time positions, or to obtain other positions, often lower-paying ones, that have the requisite flexibility they require.

While groups like NOW nominally support the idea of accommodation, they and other feminists have done almost nothing to validate child-raising as a legitimate—and often superseding—demand upon a working woman's time. Instead, they focus on the "inequality" of the child-care (or, more broadly, "caregiver') burden because it more often falls upon women. While NOW harps upon the "economic injustice" of the role, however, it does not present any compelling case *in favor of* unequal treatment in order to assist working mothers. Too often, the primary ideas it puts forward to "help" working mothers and their families is to promote government-funded day-care, day-care regulations, licensing for day-care operators, mandated "disability" time off for pregnant women, an expansion of other benefits, or some other mandate that "counts" caregivers in the economic equation. And while some of these ideas are good, almost none approach the issue from the standpoint that there are enormous social benefits to be derived from supporting and nurturing the relationship between mothers and their own children. For example, NOW tries to push a "Women-Friendly Workplace" pledge on companies which focuses less on the importance of family to working women and more on the promotion of a leftist political agenda. Thus, only one of its eleven itemized bullet points even mentions the accommodations of flex-time or job-sharing—and only as two suggested possibilities on a laundry-list of other "family friendly" policy suggestions like paid sick leave. To put this in perspective, NOW dedicates one entire bullet point for its "Women-Friendly Workplace" to guaranteeing the freedom to unionize, another to extending employee benefits to same-sex couples, and yet another to making sure that health plans provide reproductive services including, of course, abortion.

The lack of attention given to this issue as an overall feminist concern is a serious oversight—a glaring one, in fact—given the fact that the compromises women make with regard to their careers after bearing children is probably one of the most significant factors contributing to key issues feminists claim to care about, such as pay disparity and the infamous glass ceiling. More radical feminists, like Susan Faludi, simply dismiss the dilemma as non-existent, claiming that working mothers have no interest in staying at home and that the disparity problems can be blamed solely upon sexist discrimination. And while NOW, in contrast, correctly recognizes that working mothers are striving for a suitable work-family balance, it seems overly obsessed with the idea of "economic justice," as though what is really bothering most women is that motherhood does not provide a paycheck.

Feminists, as a rule, refuse to take the position that motherhood should warrant a special status by women, men, employers, and the government. Instead, they adhere to the idea that women should be treated exactly the same as men in the employment realm. NOW even implies that the problems faced by women in this regard can be partially remedied by forcing the government to classify motherhood and other unpaid care-giving responsibilities (such as for elderly parents) as though they are jobs. Even when feminists lobby, their demands for special benefits are put in neutral terms—that is, to apply to both men and women—even though it is abundantly clear that the benefits they seek are directly aimed at helping women with children. In other words, they haven't the courage or forthrightness to acknowledge what everyone knows is true—that is, that *women both need and want to take care of their own young children*—because it undermines the "equality" pretense that children are not a particularized concern of women.

While NOW at least recognizes the reality that mothers are generally not in the same position as fathers (although they are bothered by that fact), it fails to appreciate what is really at play. For many working women, the issue is not that motherhood does not pay or provide benefits, but that there are so few attractive employment options remaining once they conclude that their children merit a higher personal priority than their careers. *This* is the problem that forces women into less challenging, less upwardly mobile, and lower-paying jobs—*not* discrimination and *not* lazy husbands. By not focusing diligently upon expanding the options available *specifically for mothers*, particularly for ambitious, intelligent mothers, feminism sells short the very women it once sought to support and advance. Unfortunately, many women seem convinced that the feminist position—that is, that mothers cannot or should not merit separate treatment—is both legitimate and rational. But it is not.

In 1997, Christine Wiebe wrote an article on parenthood and medical residency in the American College of Physicians publication *ACP Observer*. In it, she points out the particular difficulties faced by medical residents, whose jobs have extremely demanding scheduling requirements. In the article, a female resident explained how difficult it is to cope with having a baby and the demands of residency, and her story highlights the unreasonableness of the position that employers—and employees—must operate on a system that is blind to the demands of motherhood. On the one hand, she complained that returning to her third year of residency only eight weeks after having a baby was too short a time: she felt distracted and thought "there is no way anyone can be 100 percent right after having a child." While she did not know how much time off would have been sufficient for her, she began to recommend to other residents that new mothers should take at least three months off. But at the same time she conceded her own ambivalence about returning to work so soon, she also complained that the administration raised the issue of her child's birth in assessing her commitment to the job, since she had been named as chief resident for the following year: "I thought I was getting scrutinized unfairly."

Well, which is it: did motherhood affect her dedication to her job or not? In short, she had been persuaded by feminist hard-liners that she must dig in her heels when her employer dared question her, as a new mother, about her ability to dedicate sufficient attention to the considerable demands of her position. Yet, as a mother, she fully admitted that having a baby impacted her ability to focus on her career. By championing only the idea of workplace "equality," and failing to stand up for what motherhood means to women, feminism encourages this contradictory attitude, common among working women like this doctor. And it is, unfortunately, a necessary hypocrisy: her employer provided no middle ground in which she could admit the very real concerns of trying to balance the demands of her career with the demands of new motherhood. She had to either deny the existence of any misgivings or risk her current and future career prospects.

In that same article, another resident pointed out that, in working ten-hour shifts, she had little time to spend with her baby, and had to rearrange her schedule with her employer far in advance. While her employer was able to accommodate many of her needs by assignments that did not involve on-call work for the first month and by making available on-site day-care, she confessed that she spent little time with her daughter and even less with her husband. Yet another resident was stretched to the limit by the demands of residency and new motherhood. She decried the "male-dominated" culture of her employer, complaining that they prejudiced women by claiming, "They would never make you chief resident if you had a baby because they would think the job was not your top priority." Yet she goes on to admit that she was at one point tempted to quit altogether, was conflicted about having to give up breast-feeding when she was placed on a 36-hour critical care rotation, and eventually switched to dermatology because, as the article explains, it was "less time-intensive and more accommodating to her family priorities."

These cases are hardly isolated. Working mothers are forever being forced to adopt the pretense with their employers that their child-rearing responsibilities do not impact their jobs or their career choices, yet privately make innumerable sacrifices and compromises in their careers in their quest to be good mothers. Some women avoid raising the issue with employers out of fear that voicing their quite legitimate concerns will blacken the impression their employers have of them. But avoiding the issue can have worse consequences. For example, if a mother shows a distinct lack of interest in a promotion—because the new job will require more travel or longer hours—her employer may have a worse impression: that she simply lacks the ambition or confidence to move upward. Even employers who are willing to accommodate a particular employee end up pretending that the special treatment is not related to motherhood, because that, too, would be viewed by others as discrimination. Both mothers and employers are forced to pretend that motherhood is a neutral employment issue, when everyone knows it is not. By failing to confront the issue head-on, working mothers and employers purposefully avoid discussing the possibilities and compromises from which they both might benefit.

Although there are a few companies that consciously and openly foster a family-friendly culture, those employers are rare. So while feminists harp about the pay disparity between men and women, they perpetuate a system that encourages working mothers to exacerbate that disparity. Plenty of working women crave professional challenges, promotions, and higher pay, but they refuse to sacrifice their families in order to keep or obtain the positions that offer them.

Two years after Christine Wiebe's article was published, Deborah Gesensway wrote another article for *ACP-ASIM Observer* on the difficulties faced by mothers working in medicine. As she explained, many women found that they had to take non-traditional jobs in medicine, because the traditional models simply provided no feasible accommodations for a sound work-family balance. A study published in the *Annals of Internal Medicine* found that women with children worked fewer hours, were published less often, and were slower to advance in their careers—but not just compared to men: the results were as compared to childless women, as well. In short, mothers' careers were stalled.

This should not come as a surprise to anyone who gives the matter serious thought. The fact is, *children have uncompromising needs that cannot be ignored by working mothers*. No matter how much feminists want to work toward or encourage the mechanization of child-rearing, family responsibilities simply cannot be shunted off like other domestic duties such as cleaning the house and cooking meals. There is no such thing as take-out child-raising, day-care notwithstanding; raising a child is not simply another household chore. As Ms. Gesensway's article goes on to state, one doctor, who worked part-time, said she knew women who had quit altogether because they "simply could not find a satisfying job that would let them work the hours they needed to be able to raise a family the way they wanted to."

Frequently, the women in medicine who have successfully "mommy-tracked" (as opposed to leaving altogether) have been women who have invented their own track, often by opening a solo practice. That is because few hospitals have adopted anything like a "mommy-track" career path for the very many women doctors who would be happy to take advantage of such an option. Thus, the professional women confronted with this choice invariably suffer, either professionally or personally. And quite unfortunately, it is assuredly true that patients and society suffer the loss of very many capable, conscientious, and much-needed medical professionals, who might be happy to make their services available if there were simply a way to accommodate their family responsibilities.

Medicine, of course, is not the only profession that makes unusual demands upon time and dedication that are largely incompatible with family life. In fact, one could easily argue that even regular full-time work is largely incompatible with family life for mothers of young children, particularly for full-time work that does not conform to a standard work week. For example, even unskilled positions can be terribly prejudicial to working mothers in places like large retail establishments where the competition is stiff for available jobs. Employees who want even minor accommodations such as fixed schedules or specific days off can be seen as troublesome, and are less attractive to employers than employees who are willing to work unpopular hours or who are willing to shift schedules on short notice. Even employers who technically offer "flex-time" can be less tolerant of employees who take advantage of it; and often, there are legitimate business reasons for advancing those employees who willingly accommodate the employer's scheduling needs. And while women in these unskilled positions may have fewer concerns about upward mobility, accommodation is still a critical concern when it comes to child-raising responsibilities.

One could argue that the conflicts working mothers face are not truly an employer's problem. But forcing working mothers into the "equality" trap can frequently end up costing employers, particularly when it comes to women in highly skilled professions. In February 2007, *California Lawyer* magazine had a feature article explaining how young women were leaving large law firms in droves. According to the article, associates, in general, are leaving the big firms at an alarming rate: three-fourths are out the door within five years. And women, who make up roughly half of the associates in California, are leaving at twice the rate of their male counterparts. Why? One reason is because large law firms do not provide sufficient opportunity for these women to find a balance more conducive to family life.

Today, most large firms continue to operate on the traditional model of requiring roughly 40 billable hours per week from associates, which can often translate into 60 or more hours of actual office time. And many young women, who graduate from law school at the age of 25 and older, are not willing to put in that kind of time (and more, if they want to be on the fast track) for the six to nine years it often takes to make partner, especially when one takes into consideration the fact that those years generally coincide with the time frame in which young women get married and start families. In the article, one associate, who had asked for part-time work or a transfer out of litigation, received no response at all from her firm. She stated that she felt the firm was essentially "asking her to neglect her family, and that no amount of money was worth that" sacrifice.

As the article readily acknowledges, the women partners at these firms, now in their 50s, were the pioneers, and they sacrificed a great deal to make partner. They took all the arrows to make it easy for the next generation, and are now a bit miffed that today's young female associates do not see the point of making such a sacrifice. Instead, the new crop of women lawyers willingly forego the partnership track in favor of their families—even to the point that many are hanging out their own shingles to exercise complete control over their work schedules. The old guard is somewhat resentful that these young women are taking their opportunities for granted and cavalierly turning their backs on the opportunities the older women worked so hard to create. On the one hand, that resentment is not entirely justified; the sacrifices they made were their own choices. On the other hand, however, these courageous women are correct that there are still new frontiers for the younger ones to forge. In particular, they expressed, today's young women should be pushing for change in the old culture, and trying to introduce the idea that a better work-life balance would enable these firms to retain the sharp young female attorneys who are leaving. What is ironic is that the article did not once mention Felice Schwartz and her mommy-tracking idea, despite the fact that what these women want is the sort of flexibility that Ms. Schwartz, twenty years ago, had suggested that working women might want. Even more, despite the fact that feminists repeatedly complain about the small number of women partners at large law firms, they do not seem to acknowledge the reason: as this article baldly states, most young female associates simply choose not to stay at large law firms long enough to make partner.

Interestingly, the accounting firm Deloitte had taken Ms. Schwartz's idea and run with it back in 1993. In a concerted effort to retain women, who, just as at the law firms, were leaving before making partner, Deloitte instituted some new policies: partnerships became available to part-time employees, the firm allowed flexible hours and offered some telecommuting options, and so on. In 13 years, the firm nearly tripled its number of female partners and, what is more, the firm found that these policies actually improved their bottom line. These policies helped Deloitte to retain good employees, retain the client relationships that those good employees nurtured, and gave bright women both professional challenges and an opportunity to exercise their talents—meaning that the time and effort Deloitte spent training and mentoring were not walking out the door with the women who received them.

What these stories reveal is that it is ridiculous for women to continue to try to sustain the façade that their families mean nothing to them when they walk in the office door. They put on a brave face while their insides are churning up due to the fact that they dropped their one-year-old off at day-care that morning even though he sneezed three times and had a bit of a runny nose, or they slap their sunglasses on to cover up the fact that they cried all the way to work because their toddler sobbed "mommy, mommy" as they walked out the door of the day-care center. Similarly, it is ridiculous for employers to continue redefining job descriptions that work around an employee's schedule under the pretense that it has nothing to do with the fact that the employee in question has a family she needs to take care of and will walk out the door unless accommodations are made. The bottom line is that women with children, especially infants and toddlers, are perfectly good employees: they just need, *not want, but need*, to be able to dedicate sufficient time to their families.

For too long, women have labored under the delusion that feminism serves their professional interests by forcing them into playing this ridiculous shell game called "equality." Frankly, there is no *need* to keep playing it. If women truly had confidence in their own value and capabilities, they would approach this issue with a clear and candid understanding of what life reasonably requires—and so would their employers. At some point, women must acknowledge their very real—and monumentally important— need to attend to the interests of their own children regardless of their careers. Women should not adopt the pretense, for purposes of politics, that their own children are never a part of their job considerations, at the same time they twist themselves into knots to try to make their jobs accommodate their families' demands. It is time women truly stood up for actual women, and not for a political illusion.

When working mothers need to pay more attention to *time* considerations than *job* considerations, employers lose good employees. Women either resign or may demote themselves into positions where their most valuable skills will add nothing to the bottom line. It is a lose-lose proposition. Unless there is a legitimate and acknowledged route for women to openly and forthrightly accommodate their child-raising responsibilities into their career demands, this ridiculous pattern will continue.

Yet, for the most part, Felice Schwartz's sympathetic and wise suggestion continues to be soundly rejected by feminists. For example, Susan Faludi simply states that sitting down with employers to discuss maternity plans is a blatant violation of Title VII of the Civil Rights Act, end of discussion. The same feminists who lobbied to extend employer benefits to same-sex partners of employees are happy to force employers to accommodate their employee's sexual orientation, but they are not willing to force employers to accommodate the needs of their employee's family obligations. What does that say about their priorities?

It is difficult to sympathize with feminists who loudly complain about the pay disparity between men women when feminism has done little of practical value to protect the income strength of scores of women who are working mothers. With so few options available, working mothers who take time off or move down or sideways in their careers do not just sacrifice present income and near-term advancement, and neither do they simply delay their advancement. These women actually move *backward* in their careers, so that if and when they reach a point where they can shift their allocation of time (such as when their youngest child begins school full-time), they have to invest a significant amount of time in their jobs simply to get back to where they were before they changed career gears. In many ways, the feminist position is a slap in the face to the very women that they tell us they champion: the women who strive for success, the ones who are unwilling to accept failure either as a parent or as a professional.

Moreover, the paranoid fear that "mommy-tracking" options open the door for employers to discriminate against women is based upon the unfounded and frankly insulting supposition that employers are just itching for an opportunity to fire or demote women which, in turn, suggests that the feminists believe that women really aren't cutting it in the business world. But the reality is just the opposite: employers know that it is foolish to let good employees go, and women have demonstrated the value of their contributions to business time and again.

Another aspect of the "equality trap" is that it has, in a way, pitted one group of women against another. Working mothers who cannot keep up with their male or childless female colleagues find themselves strung out and exhausted, resentful of their colleague's ability to field assignments and responsibilities that require additional sacrifices of time, knowing that no matter how bright and capable they are, they simply cannot compete and will not be able to move ahead. Either that, or they go ahead and compete, then beat themselves up for neglecting their families, blaming every one of their children's problems or mishaps on their own failure to dedicate enough time and energy to them. Alternatively, every time a capable working mother gets a break from an employer by getting a less demanding workload, a flexible schedule, or a day off to care for a sick child, other employees— men and women—feel a niggling resentment of what they regard as favoritism. When the employer-employee relationship labors under the "equality" illusion, this resentment is quite understandable. But the problem could be avoided if motherhood were recognized for what it is.

At some point, people—feminists included—need to acknowledge that motherhood is a demanding and important responsibility, and that caring for babies and young children is a responsibility that primarily falls upon mothers precisely because their natures are different from a man's. This is not to say that there are not men who may be perfectly capable of nurturing young children, or that all women are maternal, but exceptions do not disprove the rule. Feminists should not get away with the hypocritical stance that women are fundamentally different from men, but nevertheless possess no natural inclinations toward caring for children. Until women stand up for other women, and unite in the recognition of their distinct role as mothers, there is little hope for a brighter future for women as a whole. Like it or not, women, not men, are mothers, and *good mothers care about their children*.

Chapter Fourteen: The Child-Care "Problem"

In order to raise children with equality, we must take them away from families and communally raise them.

--Mary Jo Bane

In the absence of any widespread availability of mommy-tracking opportunities, and, to a large extent, even if such opportunities were widely available, day-care continues to be a critical concern to working mothers. While most mothers, working or not, readily sympathize with the goals of groups like NOW for things like more protective daycare regulations and minimum standards for providers, the fact is that many women with children are not merely concerned with the quality of available day-care. To a large extent, they are also concerned with the fact that, because of their need to bring in an income, they are bound to *require* quality daycare.

Once you have children, it is abundantly clear that *someone* has to be around to raise them. And a question that troubles working mothers is: who is the best person to do it? The truth is, many mothers sincerely and fervently believe that *they* are. So, while they do worry about the day-care options available, many of them would frankly welcome an additional option: the opportunity to raise their children themselves.

Before discussing this issue further, however, it is necessary to comment on the fact that many feminists tend to resent the idea that it is usually mothers, rather than fathers, who confront the child-care problem. This is occasionally fashioned into the argument that men, particularly male legislators, are a bunch of uncaring clods. Even putting aside the fact that part of the reason is that there are so many single mothers, that is simply not true. Plenty of fathers take their parental responsibilities seriously. But mothers have a more symbiotic relationship with babies and toddlers, simply by nature's design. The reason women generally feel that it is their careers, and not their husbands' careers, which primarily compete with parenthood is because they are the ones who feel the greatest pull of a child's needs, particularly in a child's infancy. The ones urging women to quit their careers and stay at home with the children are often women themselves. And before any feminists take umbrage at the idea that women are naturally more inclined to care for young children, it should be pointed out that feminism implicitly validates this perspective by asserting ownership of the child-care issue. If a men's group took on this issue, feminists would most likely lash back by telling them that, being men, they had not the faintest idea what children or their mothers needed.

In addition, something must be said regarding husbands who *do* want their wives to stay at home with the children: why is this seen by feminists as offensive or oppressive? It should not come as a surprise that a man would want his children to be raised and taken care of by his own wife, the children's own mother, rather than by some stranger. Rather than an affront to his wife, this desire should be seen as a testament to the amount of respect and love a man has for his wife and the amount of love and concern he has for his own children. And while such a shift would undoubtedly have long term impacts upon a mother's career aspirations, for a family, it is not a question of what is best for one person, but what is best for the family as a whole—and not just "best" in an economic sense. This is not to say that women *must* accede to their husband's wishes in this regard, but it is troublesome that working mothers are urged by the feminists to regard such a desire by a husband as demeaning or insulting. If "modern" "liberated" women who have successful careers resent such a request, it might explain why some husbands tread lightly in expressing themselves with regard to the day-care question, and why they might leave the decision in the hands of their wives— who, in turn, may then accuse their husbands of being uninvolved or uncaring. Encouraging women to make "the personal the political" too often has its own backlash effect.

But getting back to the issue more directly, feminists tend to discourage the choice of women to stay at home, believing that this causes women to have "lesser" lives than those that involve careers. While women who decide to stay home with their children certainly can miss the professional challenges of an interesting career and clearly sacrifice professional opportunities, most recognize the trade-off for what it is—*and still choose it.* And while feminists seem to resent the idea that women do not always attempt to "have it all," such as when NOW's then-President Kim Gandy's expressed disappointment (and suspected foul play) when ABC News anchor Elizabeth Vargas resigned upon expecting her second child, sensible women recognize that *no one* really has it all—or, at least, not all at the same time. Even the men who supposedly "had it all" were often absentee parents who relied heavily upon their stay-at-home wives for bringing up their children. No matter which way you slice it, something gives, and the something that gives is either parenting or career.

The choice between continuing to work or quitting to stay at home is a difficult one, both emotionally and financially. For single mothers, of course, there is usually no choice at all. But for the mothers who have the luxury of choice, the ones who choose parenting know that they are giving up both income and income potential, and the ones who give up a greater share of parenting know that they are making a pragmatic choice, the emotional costs of which they usually try to offset in other ways. Tellingly, however, the feminists' political weight is put behind only the latter choice by promoting better day-care, which they then cast as a "family friendly" effort. But how is always favoring mothers placing their children in the care of someone else truly friendly to the family?

The reality is that there are a number of legislative options that would be more "family friendly" if feminism supported women staying at home with their young children as much as they supported women in the paid workforce. For example, a significant increase in the per-child tax deduction might enable families to gain sufficient economic leeway to consider the possibility of one parent being able to stay home. It could even be a graduated deduction, that would provide *higher* deductions for children below school-age—when children need more attention, when the parents' earning power is usually weaker, when parent-child bonding is so essential, and, incidentally, when parents are so much more (and quite justifiably) concerned about the capabilities and quality of outside care-givers. It is true that not every couple would take advantage of such a policy to enable one parent to stay home, but even a modest chunk taken out of the demand market for good child-care would ease the strains on the already scarce supply.

As discussed previously, giving working mothers mommy-tracking options like job-sharing and flex-time are valuable. But the truth is that those sorts of ideas are aimed primarily at the upper economic strata of working mothers—women with professional degrees or management careers, such that holding steady to retain earning power is a concern for those women who want to resume their upward career tracks when the brunt of their child-raising obligations ease up. But to the working waitress or assembly worker, taking time out to raise a child or children is not a real career-buster. On the contrary, taking time off to raise a child *is* the luxury. And this is where the real benefit of policies like a high per-child tax deduction could benefit women and their families the most.

Unlike legislated policies, such as mandating that employers provide paid time off, with their usual bureaucratic menu of exceptions, qualifications, and so on, a tax deduction is available no matter the nature of the job, no matter the size of the employer, and no matter who is doing the earning. Married mothers in the lower economic classes might find that a high deduction would completely compensate for the offsetting loss of income, and allow families to live on one salary. And while single mothers would still have to work, it would greatly relieve them of the financial pressures that force them to work longer hours or at more stressful jobs in order to provide the income they need to remain financially afloat.

In contrast, the day-care option is simply one more significant expense placed upon working families and, like most services, the wealthy can always afford better care. And current tax policy hardly provides any assistance. Not only is calculating the child-care tax credit a fairly complicated affair, in the end, it usually amounts to a measly $50 to $100 per month break that does virtually nothing to alleviate the true cost of outside child-care. When you take into account that decent care for an infant or toddler—and by decent, that means clean, qualified, and safe, where even a half-conscientious parent would feel relatively comfortable leaving his or her children—costs many hundreds per month (in the northern California area, over $700 per month, and usually significantly more for an infant and even more if you live in an urban locale where the cost of living is higher), the dependent care credit barely makes a dent. Consequently, when parents pay for child-care, the net amount of income they bring in is appreciably reduced, so that many women (or men, as the case may be) who opt to continue working rather than stay at home—because of the need for supplemental income—end up netting maybe a half or two-thirds of what their childless co-workers make. And, of course, the numbers get even more dismal the more children there are in any kind of day-care.

A woman may be netting a very respectable $4,000 or $5000 per month, but if she and her husband are paying $1500 (or more) in daycare and they only get a $70 dollar break on that amount due to the dependent care credit, her income becomes appreciably reduced. Add to that the fact that the couple still has to carry out family and household chores, spend time racing around town to drop off and pick up the children, take sick and vacation days off to care for sick children, the additional non-deductible costs of gas, dry-cleaning and other job wardrobe needs, the purchase of more expensive restaurant or other prepared foods, additional car maintenance, plus the fact that they only get to spend time with the children on nights and weekends when they also have to catch up on housework, and suddenly the mother is left wondering why on earth she is busting her back to let other people raise her children while she is earning what amounts to a paltry stipend. The "benefits" of working become even less alluring when you factor in the fact that her salary, combined with her husband's, may be elevating them into a higher tax bracket which further reduces the relative income of the family when she compares working to staying at home.

Groups like NOW are not lobbying for change that makes this sort of day-care dilemma a non-dilemma. Instead, they are lobbying for things like forcing taxpayers to fund one year off at full-time pay for federal employees to stay at home with a child following child-birth, as in Sweden. But while this policy may sound nice, its aim is more political than familial. Right on its face, it is not clear why taxpayers should fund exorbitant benefits for federal employees that no other employees in America have, which suggests that this ploy is merely the tip of the iceberg: this is a first step in pushing this same benefit onto private employers or, worse, taxpayers. One wonders how NOW imagines that private employers can easily bear the cost of paying people for contributing nothing to their bottom line. After all, Sweden's program, along with its other progressive socialist programs, is funded by a 32% corporate tax, a 30% to 60% individual tax, a 32% payroll tax, and a 25% value added tax. If NOW were truly interested in families, they might stop to consider that these same parents (not to mention employers) would be a lot better off if our government simply gave parents a meaningful and significant tax break for every minor child at home, and let parents *fund their own time off for however long they pleased based on their own choices*. Moreover, giving those women who want to stay at home the ability to do so would free up a portion of the job market for those whose choices are not dictated (or chosen) by family demands.

It is concededly true that the policy suggested here would demonstrate favoritism toward families with children. One could also argue that, if people don't like the current economics of the situation, they should not have children. But the "maternal card" cannot be played only whenever some tax-cut, spending cut, or defense authorization theoretically takes food out of the mouths of children or, perhaps, their welfare-reliant mothers. At some point, the feminist movement should play the maternal card to stand for the proposition that women not only *have* children, but *want to have* those children, and *want to be able to spend time* with those children. An increase in the child deduction would favor families with children, but that's because our society *should* favor families with children. Well-brought-up, well-cared for, and happy children should not be a luxury, an extravagance enjoyed only by the very wealthy, particularly when the welfare of the country overall depends upon how many well-brought-up, well-cared for, and happy people populate it.

Regardless of whether the government adopts the policy suggested here or any other, America had better recognize at some point that the welfare of children is the key to the future of this country, and that loving families—and particularly, loving, caring, and *present* families—provide the best environment in which to raise them if the country wants to be populated by good citizens. The feminist position is frequently nothing more than a dressed up version of the recycled leftist canon that the state should be raising children, away from the nefarious influences of their parents, whose love and indulgence is only a distraction from (and in competition with) "more important" societal concerns with which these children ought to be indoctrinated. Even NOW's "one-year-off" policy is not a matter of freeing up families to pursue their own priorities, but a mandated entitlement program of government "benevolence" that exists, by the way, only so long as, and subject to all the conditions under which, that government shows a willingness to bestow it.

Perhaps the most important aspect of this issue, though, is that day-care simply does not supply a comprehensive remedy for the conflicts and difficulties working mothers face. The truth is, the feminists' unshakeable faith in "quality" day-care is unfounded, no matter how many licensing regulations get passed. The primary problem is that if, as feminists often contend, mothers do not, or need not, care enough for their own children to stay at home to raise them, how is it possible to find enough *other people* who *will* willingly, happily, and competently raise them? The market is simply not overflowing with a supply of men and women who can capably provide tender loving care, attention, affection, and support to an assortment of children to whom they are completely unrelated for a lousy eight dollars an hour.

No matter which way you cut it, children need care, and there is a shortage of superior, affordable care available—whether that affordability means outside help or self-help. Workable solutions can be found, but feminists do not seem to be interested in any plan that allows or expands the option of staying at home if women so choose. In effect, the feminist agenda creates a self-fulfilling portrait of American womanhood: by foreclosing for many working mothers the option of staying at home with their children or at least mommy-tracking, it is easy for feminists to claim that *women really do not want to stay at home.* By demonstrating that most women return to their jobs after having children, they can validate the claim that women would much rather mix it up with their colleagues at the office day in and day out than raise their children. They can deny the existence of the maternal character, and bolster their own version of history: men oppressed women by making them "breed," when in reality women would much rather have ventured out to lead armies and found companies and operate earth-moving machinery.

Again, it becomes apparent that modern feminism is not directed at allowing women to determine their own priorities and interests and to enable them to pursue them. Sadly, it is not even about giving women who want to "have it all" the means to achieve that goal. The modern feminist ideal is not so much a real woman but a political construct, an intellectually conceived figment that the feminists can define and describe, but who does not have flesh and blood and normal feminine traits or feelings. But real women need more than that, particularly when they find out that trying to emulate that mythic feminist ideal isn't very glamorous or even remotely gratifying.

As stated above, there is nothing wrong, in principle, with the fact that mothers may want or need to work. But one cannot, like the feminists, simply expect that the effort to shift mothers away from childcare responsibilities and into the workforce comes with no consequences and no problems. As explained previously, raising a child is not just another household chore like watering the houseplants. For a movement to legitimately claim that it represents women, any solutions it proposes must appreciate what the realities are: the causes, the challenges, the goals, and the potential remedies—but all within the framework of what is both *feasible and desirable for actual women*. Simply telling mothers: "Well, just hire someone to care for the children!" does nothing to resolve the very serious and legitimate concerns of mothers and fathers who, one might imagine, have a tad more than a passing interest in who may be watching and teaching and guiding their children. Parents can't just shrug off mistakes and misjudgments when it comes to their children's care. Feminism needs to be interested in *what is actually required* to make motherhood work, not just interested in *what they want* to work, insofar as their proposed solutions might dovetail nicely with their political ideals.

There is no question that day-care is a social necessity, particularly for single mothers who have no choice but to work to support their families. But for intact families, mothers would be better served if day-care were an option that gave women maximum flexibility to fashion their family lives to suit their own priorities. In particular, the current scarcity of affordable, quality day-care for young children is a problem that many women face, particularly women in the lower economic strata. It should not merely be well-heeled professional women or couples who have the luxury of choice or flexibility. Motherhood is not only a *legitimate* responsibility for women to fulfill, but a *vital, honorable, respectable, and necessary* one, regardless of whatever other responsibilities women may bear or undertake. Mothers understand that caring for children is never a job. It is, instead, an entrustment.

SECTION FIVE: MEN

Chapter Fifteen: A Few Random Thoughts About Men . . . and Women

> *I feel that "man-hating" is an honorable and viable political act, that the oppressed have a right to class-hatred against the class that is oppressing them.*
>
> *--Robin Morgan*

It is true that our society, historically, has glorified certain aspects of what feminists label the male-dominated or patriarchal structure of western culture. But in questing after similar glory, the feminist movement did not really do itself any favors by encouraging women to buy into those same priorities. After all, the mere fact that, today, women *can* do many of the jobs that men do does not amount to a contention that woman *ought to* or *need to* do such things. Oddly, at the same time the feminists like to trumpet the dissimilarities between men and women, they nevertheless have sought to thrust women into historically masculine arenas—politics, business, and so on—and under the same set of rules. But why? Why is it so important to modern feminists that women become, to state it plainly, what men have been?

The feminists display a sort of multiple personality disorder. They decry a social order formed along patriarchal lines, but they also want to be part of that traditional men's network: they want women to work for a living, to be political leaders, to be news anchors, to box, to play professional sports, to sleep around, and, probably, to let their legs get hairy. In addition, they frequently look down upon women who fulfill the traditional roles of wife and mother; in fact, it is sometimes harder to find any *men* who have as low an opinion of wives and mothers as some feminists do. Nonetheless, feminists also argue that women are entirely different from men. They proclaim that women do not subscribe to men's methods of gauging value or measuring accomplishment or solving problems, and they bristle at the way men recognize and laud each other's achievements. At the same time, they seem to lust after that same public recognition, as though it not only *does* constitute a validation of one's life, but *ought to* constitute a validation of one's life.

It is a strange and deluded feminism that exalts the role of men in nearly every capacity, especially when you consider that in the cosmic scheme of things, men's lives, throughout history, have not exactly been a walk in the park. The responsibilities and burdens men have borne may seem glorious when reading about famous figures in a history book, but for every man who accomplished great things, there were millions who led (and lead) humble and obscure lives, and many who have ended up dying for all those great men—not to mention all the infamous men whose bids for greatness ended up instead with lives lost in disgrace, wretchedness, or agony.

Even when it comes to the everyday male, feminism has overly romanticized the male role of breadwinner. It is easy to understand the frustration felt by Betty Friedan and other housewives at the lack of opportunities available to women, but the 1950's version of the middle-class American male had just as few options. He probably also lay in bed at night with the same question his antsy wife confronted: is this all there is? Women may have grumbled about the smugness of self-important men with driving ambitions who spent 60 to 70 hours every week working their way up to CEO, and who neglected their families yet achieved their professional aspirations with a beautiful beaming wife and perfect children by their side. But most men never reached those career pinnacles. Surely *somebody* must have been mopping floors, counting beans, selling cars, flipping burgers, digging ditches, embalming bodies, and waiting tables. Maybe it wasn't so wonderful for a man to work like a dog eight to ten hours a day at a barely satisfying and not-so-well paying job, particularly if he came home to a nagging, bored, and dissatisfied wife; to children he spent too little time with, and who grew up while he spent his life at the office; a lawn that perpetually needed mowing; an endless stream of bills for a car that needed a new transmission and new tires; and knowing that he would have to financially support his wife, children, lawn, car, and mortgage until the day he died.

Of course, that clichéd image of unexciting suburban middle-class family life ignores the intimate relationships and the tender, stirring motivations that were really at play—all the reasons that men and women willingly and happily shouldered the more mundane realities of getting by both then as well as today. And the truth is, it is those small but monumentally important personal matters that constitute the real sum of a life: not careers, not awards, not bank accounts. In the end, a satisfying life well-lived constitutes the real reward for one's efforts—whether recognized publicly or privately.

This is why it is so tedious that feminism continues to entertain the idea that somehow glory awaits womanhood via the working, politically powerful female. Make no mistake, it is a good thing that women today have tremendous opportunities before them. The freedom to obtain an education and the opportunity to pursue jobs that are challenging and interesting and that engage one's mind and talent are wonderful benefits for women and wonderful achievements for the women's movement. But this expansion of opportunities does not somehow transform the world; humankind is not on the verge of some great feminist metamorphosis into an Amazonian utopia. The bottom line is: a job is still just a job. If a woman decides to quit her job and stay at home, what is it to feminists? Does a woman who acquires money or power necessarily make the world a better place than the woman who works for nothing but the well-being and happiness of others? Hardly. Feminism has lost sight of actual women in its quest to reinvent womanhood.

On so many issues, feminism does not seem to know where it is going or what it is doing or why it is doing it. Feminism is so intent upon its narrow-minded iconoclasm that it does not seem to ever question the larger issue of what it means to be female or even what it means to be human. And feminists have very peculiar ideas about what it means to be a man.

It seems that at the root of all their bashing of marriage, of motherhood, of society, of the world . . . is the feminists' irrational anger and resentment of men. The term "irrational" is used not because men are angels, but because human beings are human beings. It is ridiculous to claim that the evils of the world exist because men, rather than women, have stood in the positions of power. Feminists seem to resent the fact that men are physically stronger, perhaps recognizing that, in generations past, that very strength is what naturally bestowed upon men their leadership role—politically, personally, and socially. But that strength is also what helped people to survive, including women, and that strength is what built the world that we have. There is not much profit in wondering what the world might otherwise be, and there is even less profit in contending, with no foundation whatsoever, that our world would somehow be superior had our history not been our history. Camille Paglia, who may be described as an independent feminist, put it even more bluntly: "If civilization had been left in female hands, we would still be living in grass huts."

For American women especially, even a moment's reflection indicates that, if all that masculine strength were truly focused upon the subjugation of women, women would certainly have experienced far greater evils than a lack of equal opportunity and a future limited to being a bored housewife. Even a brief glimpse at competing cultures throughout history can give us a fair idea of what people are capable of when they are truly intent upon domination and oppression. Just as an example, the Taliban regime in Afghanistan is a prime example of how a culture can relegate women to the lowliest rung of the social ladder (if not the lowliest rung of the living beings ladder). And the communist Chinese, whom the feminists sometimes tout for their recognition of treating women as "equal" to men in the workforce (for what that's worth in such a regime), nevertheless subject women to forced abortions, abort or abandon their female babies, or, if a daughter reaches marriageable age, essentially sell them to meet the growing demand for women in a demographic in which men (who could have guessed?) greatly outnumber women. Given that not a single society in this world has honored women more than western Judeo-Christian culture, it is somewhat difficult for many American women to work themselves up into an appropriate frame of mind that is fertile for feminist man-hating propaganda.

As stated before, it is not that women must accept the *status quo*. But change simply for the sake of change has little value, and you cannot change the world into something that is unrelated to reality just because it sounds like a nifty idea. Technology and economic changes have created a society in which physical strength is no longer a necessary attribute for survival; history has conspired to allow women to step up into roles that were previously unattainable, and that fact is worth celebrating. But it hardly renders men useless or irrelevant. Just as the feminine perspective and feminine character can contribute good things to the future we create, so can masculine perspectives and masculine character. If we choose to credit men for all the evil that has been perpetrated in the world, it is beyond argument that we must also, then, credit them for all the progress that has been made in the world. After all, if men had been so intent upon oppression, they certainly could have continued to deny women even the right to own property. But men are neither angels nor demons; they are simply men.

Even more, one cannot help but feel that feminism's attempt to relegate men to the sidelines, by claiming that they are unnecessary or bad, tends to create a self-fulfilling prophecy. By belittling fatherhood and fathers, by rebuking men as uncaring brutes, by telling men that their wives, ex-wives, and sexual partners do not need them for anything but sperm-donations, the feminists are essentially justifying and endorsing the basest inclinations of the male animal. When a man tries to take a leadership role in his family, feminists bash them because they say they are perpetuating the patriarchal structure exemplified by western history and the Christian faith, in which men deem themselves the protectors and providers of their more vulnerable women and children. This, for feminists, is a stance that is too horrific to tolerate. At the same time, if men are unfeeling cads who abandon their wives and offspring, or never marry so that they can behave like frivolous playboys, or who are violent, the feminists act as though this is simply men acting like men. What have real men got to lose? There is no way for them to win. Feminism does not seem to acknowledge that many men are, and many men are quite capable of being, wholesome and respectful at the same time they can be strong and masculine. Men might just as well take feminists at their word and behave like louts or rogues.

The only men who seem to universally merit honorable mention within the feminist outlook are gay men, or men who are effeminate, weak, subservient, and timid—the sort of men one too often encounters in hip urban retail establishments. (Although, as mentioned in Section Two, feminists do seem to support politically powerful men, regardless of behavior, so long as they toe the feminist party line.) But men of that variety offer little to the many women, particularly those strong and intelligent women, who prefer men who are both intellectually and physically stimulating. Feminists, in a juicy game of turnabout, may want men who are doormats, with nothing to recommend them but blind adoration and lap-dog subservience, but is that what most women want? Even a cursory observation of society does not suggest so, particularly when it comes to women with self-respect—and who seek respect from others.

Correspondingly, for a woman who wholeheartedly adopts the feminist mindset, it is hard to imagine what she has to offer, romantically speaking, to any man who is himself successful, capable, strong, and confident. By this, we are not talking about women who are otherwise intelligent and professionally successful, but women who are die-hard feminists: resentful of men, single-mindedly focused on personal advancement, scornful of the role of wife and/or mother, and disdainful of all cultural traditions and conventions.

As a general matter, men and women still want men and women to behave like men and women, no matter how much the feminists don't like it or, more accurately, won't admit it. For example, while one can hardly hold up Hollywood as exemplifying what modern life does or ought to look like, it generally tends to reflect popular opinion. And the fact is, despite efforts to change public perception, popular male and female film roles still tend to adhere to traditional role-playing, and successful actors and actresses typically reflect idealized images of masculine men and feminine women (even though, as we cannot avoid learning in the supermarket check-out line, their actual appearances and, of course, actual lives, are something less than ideal, let alone enviable). While some of this is marketing, no amount of honest soul-searching of our truer natures would make James Bond more appealing to either men or women if he prevailed, not by being a handsome masculine powerhouse, but a skinny, pasty-faced, effeminate pushover who was nevertheless smart and had great fashion sense. And few men are interested in dating or working for James Bond's new boss, the feminized "M," however smart, assertive, and capable she may be.

At some point, the feminists have to accept that they are, in fact, women, and to accept that men are, in fact, men, and *to like it that way*. Accordingly, this section discusses some of the peculiar ways in which feminism has misunderstood men in its unabashed zeal to condemn them. In particular, it discusses how feminism has tried to de-sex men by forcing men into behaving as though a woman's sex does not affect them at the same time that women claim a right to exploit their own sexuality. It discusses how sexuality necessarily plays a role in how men and women relate to one another, and discusses how no amount of futzing with the language to eliminate "sexist" terms can somehow make men and women "equal." Finally, it discusses how feminism has overplayed its hand by demanding, irrationally, that men and women somehow turn off their sexual natures within the office environment.

Chapter Sixteen: Men Generally Act Like Men, and Women Act Like Women

> *On the one hand, we'll never experience childbirth. On the other hand, we can open all our own jars.*
>
> *--Bruce Willis*

The modern feminist movement has generally done a lousy job of figuring out how its own positions on social issues would play out in the public arena and, more particularly, how its positions would play out among men. This stems from a blindness feminists seem to have as to what drives men at the same time that they pretend to understand it. It is a truism that men and women are vastly different, or, at least, is should be a truism. But the feminists do not seem to fully appreciate what that means.

I do not profess to be the lone woman in the world who truly understands how men think. Far from it. But a woman does not necessarily have to understand men; she simply has to appreciate and accept them for who and what they are. After all, one does not need to understand how a DVD player works in order to watch a movie. In the context of what is talked about here, the mechanics of men is more or less the same.

The answer, of course, is that men are driven by sex. Naturally, unlike in other animals, the human male sex drive is greatly moderated by intellect. But the sex drive is tremendously powerful, and, though it sounds remarkably like a crude cliché, it does not need to be treated with either school-girlish embarrassment or hyper-feminist disdain. The sex drive is a formidable motivator, as history has proven time and time again. Once you understand and appreciate this basic fact, many of the problems encountered by feminists become very easy to comprehend. Almost all social phenomena make sense when you understand how mankind's fundamental instincts manifest themselves and, further, how every culture uses social conventions to tame those instincts and channel them toward productive and beneficial ends. Or, at least, that is the hope and aim.

Stating this fact is not intended to dismiss or denigrate men, either individually or as a group. Saying that men are driven by sex is really no more significant than saying that men, as a rule, are stronger than women, or taller, or hairier. When you get down to particular men, of course, this fact is not particularly helpful in terms of predicting or even understanding specific behavior. But overall, it has a great deal of significance.

And there is, of course, a correlative: women are driven by the need to create and nurture life. As a general rule, in nature, men are necessary to create life, but women are necessary to sustain life. Of course, men and women are much more than that, but that is the basis on which you have to approach the relationship between them on a broad scale in order to understand why the feminists keep running into problems, and why they need to keep coming up with new "solutions" that seem to drive them further and further into an ever more elaborate landscape of problems as they attempt to realize their utopian ideal.

In Maureen Dowd's entertaining dissection of the sexes, *Are Men Necessary?*, she spends a great deal of time discussing the modern woman's obsession with cosmetic surgery. The discussion is both somewhat gruesome (in describing the pathetic lengths to which women—and, these days, men, as well—go to combat the ravages of time) and tremendously amusing (in revealing just how pathetically vain women have become). And in her discussion of botox, bovine collagen, liposuction, implants, and plastic surgery, she makes a statement that is profoundly odd: "Feminism has been defeated by narcissism."

But, not surprisingly, Maureen Dowd is dead wrong. Feminism *is* narcissism.

Feminism is, and wallows in, the love of self. It is precisely why modern feminists favor abortion, disfavor marriage, and support child-care. The necessary implication of these positions is that women should only think of themselves and what they want, before any other interest: before their own children, before their own husbands, before the world, before anyone. Modern feminism has done its utmost to retrain the female psyche by trying to drill into women the idea that all their nurturing, helpful, supportive, maternal, and selfless instincts are not part of their inherent nature, but are instead the vile products of oppressive and corrupt social conditioning. This mindset, one is supposed to believe, was created by men specifically and deliberately to force upon women a subservience that is, surprisingly, alien to a woman's *true* nature. This is precisely why, in feminism, there is no room for preserving any vestige of a "patriarchal" culture, notwithstanding the fact that men continue to make up roughly half of the world's population. To the feminist, all of history is irrelevant because it is tainted by this insidious stain. Instead, men are expected to wear a figurative hair-shirt in penance for this supposed crime, to meekly and willingly step aside for a millennia or two while women get to prove what a superior job they can do in running the world. In the feminist creed, self comes before any other fact.

This, of course, was not Ms. Dowd's point. She was trying to argue that the modern woman's preoccupation with physical beauty was a step backward for women, a surrender to the old idea that women should strive to be ornamental rather than substantive. But what she did not see is that even the modern woman's obsession with vanity is entirely consistent with the feminist quest for power—but not in the way that feminists might prefer. From her perspective and the perspective of the feminist movement, women are supposed to shun sex as a means to power. Instead, women are supposed to use only their brainpower, aggression, and street-smarts. But if women used only those tools, they would simply (and ineffectively) mirror the virility formula that makes men attractive to women and demonstrates a man's superiority to other men. Those character traits are not the same things that make women attractive to men or demonstrate a woman's superiority to other women. These traits are not going to lead women to becoming popular and authoritative—as feminists have found to their persistent irritation and resentment.

Feminists consistently express outrage at the fact that women are often judged on their appearances, notwithstanding the fact that, for women, appearances simply matter—*both to them and to other people*. If they did not matter, they would all shun make-up, fashion, and hairstyles. But feminists seem to think the *world should simply pretend that it does not matter*. Thus, NOW was particularly miffed that, during the long run up to the 2008 election, this factor came into play with respect to Hillary Clinton and other female politicians, such as Nancy Pelosi. NOW editorialized:

> Female politicians have long struggled with a double standard: while being criticized or perceived as "soft" or "weak" if they come across as too traditionally feminine, they are also accused of being too "hard" or "strident" if they come off as assertive and powerful — traditionally masculine attributes. While these impossible standards are being subverted by successful women politicians such as new House Speaker Nancy Pelosi, many journalists don't seem to know what to do with strong women. These professionals, who should know better, often revert to old-fashioned sexism in describing women leaders (*e.g.* denigrating women for qualities, like aggressiveness or ambition, that are seen as positive attributes in men), scrutinizing their appearance, and concentrating on their roles as dutiful wives and mothers to the exclusion of their political accomplishments and records on the issues.

> Indeed, in Pelosi's first days as Speaker of the House, The Washington Post's Style section ran an article on Nov. 10 dissecting her choice of clothing for her swearing in ceremony, in which writer Robin Givhan used the word "chic" to describe her appearance and claimed that "an Armani suit, for a woman, is a tool for playing

with the boys without pretending to be one." As Annette Fuentes responded in a Feb. 13 USA Today opinion piece, "I would wager that Pelosi is one woman who doesn't play around with anyone."

Clinton is no stranger to this kind of treatment from the press. [. . .]

Adding insult to injury, The New York Times published a Maureen Dowd piece (titled "Mama Hugs Iowa") on Jan. 31 charging that as First Lady, Clinton showed off "a long parade of unflattering outfits and unnervingly changing hairdos." So we not only have to hear about what she's wearing today, but what she wore (and how she styled her hair) in 1992. On Feb. 9, Reuters news agency reported fashion designer Donatella Versace's advice that "Hillary Clinton should tap into her feminine side and wear dresses and skirts instead of trousers."

As dismaying and tiresome as it is that journalists may focus on the picayune details of a woman politician's appearance and fashion sense, it is nevertheless silly for feminists to act as though journalists are the only ones who pay attention to these things. The fact is, people often judge women on appearances, *including most other women*. For instance, this objection to focusing on appearances did not prevent NOW from lampooning Governor Sarah Palin's appearance on its own website by suggesting her as a "horrifying" Halloween costume. The costume suggestion poked fun at her hairdo (use "lots of hairspray"), her clothing (use "a wardrobe that didn't cost $150,000"), glasses, and beauty pageant background (wear a banner that reads "Miss Real America"). Is that what NOW meant by focusing on a woman politician's "political accomplishments and records on the issues"?

The bottom line is, both men and women prefer women to demonstrate feminine attributes. And the fact that people may find traits like aggressiveness and assertiveness unbecoming in women is neither surprising nor shocking. Most women understand, instinctively, that the power equation is simply different for women and men, and it is different precisely because of sex. Power is not simply a matter of one's title or position, but of the ability to command respect and inspire obedience in others. No amount of de-sexing the language used by the press is going to make men and women react to men and women as something other than men and women. Consequently, ambitious women tend to play up their feminine strengths—that is, play the sex card—so that men will forgive or overlook a woman's aggressive and competitive drives in their subconscious lust after beauty. In short, most women understand that what gives them power over men (as well as other women) depends, to some degree, upon utilizing their sexuality to advantage.

Sex has been the basis upon which women have historically wielded power, even in the distant past. It is just that these old ways are not the ways today's feminists *want* women to have wielded it. Throughout history, women have used their sexuality as a means to power, from Cleopatra to Mata Hari. Certainly, it is desirable that women should expand their repertoire to include less sensational means, but even as *politically* powerless as they were on the world stage, women have never been just potting soil, and women have known it. Today, the endless quest to look attractive, to perpetuate the outward projection of the fertile and attractive 25-year-old woman, is part and parcel of that feminist narcissism and quest for power, whether feminists concede the point or not.

Because they are *naturally* motivated by sex, men, as a rule and to a certain degree, will be physically attracted to (and thus willing to be led by) women based upon their outward projections of fertility: attractive features, curvaceous figures, and youthfulness. This is not to say that men do not love or respect women both individually and even in the abstract for a myriad reasons that go far beyond these superficial qualities. But when it comes to instinctive *attraction*, the formula is simple. This is particularly true in arenas such as politics, where women are not relating to people on a personal level, but are, instead, relying upon the persona they project from a distance. Thus, since women only have a few short years in which to play the power game of youthful sexuality, they have embraced the alternative avenues of flattering fashion, cosmetic surgery, make-up, and a fanatical dedication to pilates and yoga to fake the advantage. It can hardly be surprising that women whose aim is the acquisition of power, feminists included, should attempt to use the advantage of sexual attraction for as long as possible to maximize their ability to wield power over others.

And while women can thus be forgiven, to some degree, for seeking to preserve a youthful appearance, there is something a little grotesque about those who cling to it as a lifeline. No matter how you cut it, even a 50 year-old beauty who "carries it well" will have a hard time competing with a 25-year old stunner in effortless possession of nature's favor. And while this means that older women may have a tougher time of it, at some point, women just have to accept themselves for what they are—and to accept men on the same terms—no matter what the fallout. Sexist or not, women cannot reasonably expect people to turn off their sexuality and judge them solely on some asexual "human" scale just because, in a libido-free meritocracy, that's how the world would work.

This is not to say that blatant sexism must be condoned, or even *any* sexism within some spheres, but it seems silly to pretend that men and women can or will at some point regard one other by some sexless measure of character. And while women of strong and commendable character or charisma can frequently overcome a disadvantage of downright unattractiveness, women are often judged by what they look like and how they present themselves—by men and women alike. At the same time, men have their own "sexist" appearance and personality hurdles to overcome. It is, unfortunately or not, the nature of the beast.

Chapter Seventeen: Men and Women at Work

I can imagine nothing worse than a man-governed world -- except a woman-governed world.

--Nancy Astor

As noted above, sexuality is part and parcel of our beings. At all ages, even though the dynamics change, it plays into how men and women deal with one another, and it always has. Despite this truth, however, feminists seem to imagine that people can simply check their sexuality at the lobby door when operating in an office environment.

This chapter discusses two issues related to the attempt to make the office environment sexless. First, it discusses the issue of harassment, and the peculiar ideas feminism has on what one can realistically expect regarding human behavior. Second, it discusses the notorious glass ceiling, the theoretical limit on the heights to which women can aspire in corporate and political America because of enduring covert sexism. Although these issues are somewhat unrelated, they are both dependent upon the feminist insistence that men and women can somehow avoid behaving like men and women.

For decades, the workplace was largely a male bastion. This is not to say that women have not always worked, particularly at the lower end of the economic spectrum, but there is no question that men held all positions of power. This meant that there was, historically, a high tolerance for crude language, lewd references, and off-color jokes within these all-male enclaves, as well as mistreatment of female underlings. The presence of these behaviors was tolerated primarily because women were not part of the management structure in which these practices thrived; moreover, women lacked the means to eliminate them. The feminist movement changed that. By the time women were "legitimately" at work—that is, women were, in large numbers, moving into higher level jobs that required a college degree and their careers were regarded as permanent rather than temporary—it was clear that something was going to have to be done if the workplace was going to be harmonious.

True sexual harassment is a serious problem, and women both inside and outside of the feminist movement have made important strides in dealing with this issue. Unfortunately, however, feminists have taken the issue to an illogical extreme, in which men are required to ignore the fact that women are women at the same time that they are supposed to be hyper-conscious of women. For example, men are discouraged from noticing a woman's shapely calf above a spike-heeled shoe, yet must be sufficiently aware of female sensibilities to realize that a female co-worker might be offended at seeing a copy of the Sports Illustrated swimsuit issue in their cubicles. Men must be aware of the female psyche, but not the female body. This is almost diametrically opposed to how men actually behave.

However, this is not to say that men should not be made to curb their baser instincts while at work. They should. But there is a problem. The problem is that at the same time they began to make a big deal about boorish, sexist, and sexually offensive office behavior, feminists were actively discouraging the idea that women should be shown any respect at all. Gentlemanly courtesies demonstrating respect, gestures such as opening doors, holding out chairs, and paying bills for women (and expecting no sexual favors in return), addressing women as Miss or Ma'am, standing up when women entered a room, refraining from using foul language in the company of women, and so on, became unacceptable "discrimination" to feminists. They encouraged women to behave and speak more like men, and to disdain behaving like ladies. Niceties shown by men toward women were seen as condescending and sexist, and feminists were ill-mannered toward men who observed these courtesies. One can only imagine the difficulty men (especially older men) encountered as the "revolution" was taking place, trying to gauge what a woman's reaction would be to the simple act of opening a door: will she smile and say "Thank you," or will she give a dirty look and ungratefully snap, "I can open a door by myself"? And if he did not open the door, a lady would be affronted by his atrocious manners and a feminist would disdainfully ignore him or give him an "I dare you" stare. It was a gamble every time. Most sensible men probably made a hasty detour every time they saw a woman approach a door just to avoid the dilemma.

Feminists may be giving themselves a pat on the back for their tireless efforts to eliminate these old-fashioned, "sexist," but perfectly decent manners, but they have now found out that manners are a necessity. Manners dictate what is appropriate to say and to do in a given setting; manners help people to get along civilly. When manners dictate behavior, people have a way of relating to one another even when communication fails. Manners not only facilitate relationships between friends, acquaintances, and colleagues, but also enable mortal enemies or strangers to capably manage the task of getting along. And manners are especially important, if not vital, to make the workplace a comfortable environment for both men and women without unseemly sexual tension. Merely working in close proximity generally provides tension enough. But while manners are essential, it is unreasonable for feminism to insist upon its convoluted standard of workplace etiquette in the midst of a culture in which the idea of imposing standards of decency between men and women has basically been exterminated.

Beginning in the 1980's, and proceeding right on up through today, in movies, on television, in books, on the radio, and everywhere else, crude language, sexually explicit banter, sexually loose behavior, and suggestive innuendo have become everyday conversation and everyday spectacles. Our culture is inundated by the airing of language and subject matter that 40 years ago never saw the light of day, but which today is unceasingly force-fed to the public, no matter how reluctant that public may be. While feminists, including NOW, have been admirably staunch in their condemnation of sexually demeaning lyrics and speech, they have not fully appreciated the connection between the coarsening of acceptable manners—including what should and should not be expressed out loud—and the problems encountered by men and women in the workplace. Despite the fact that society has virtually no standards left as to what is or is not acceptable in either manner or language (other than the politically correct taboos against racist or homophobic terms or sentiments), men are nevertheless expected to have some innate sense of exactly where the line is on acceptable workplace language and conduct. Men and women are expected to miraculously shed all of the unseemly influences that the entire outside world is forcefully thrusting upon them, and behave like well-bred Victorian gentlemen and ladies the moment their rear ends hit their ergonomically-engineered swivel chairs.

This criticism of irrationality, however, is not meant to excuse workplace harassment or misbehavior. Quite the opposite. But there must be some degree of proportion. When society is treated to gratuitous utterances of the "F" word as everyday parlance, and sexually explicit speech and conduct are regularly broadcast across the airwaves in prime-time or bluntly discussed in women's magazines, it strains credibility to assert that women do not have enough fortitude to withstand—or at least appropriately handle—the occasional lapse in judgment from a male co-worker without calling down the wrath of litigation. If women are to command respect in any sphere, it cannot be based upon codes of manner that are so utterly whimsical, in which men must treat the same woman with varying degrees of dignity depending only upon the time and place.

The level of respect to which men and women are entitled in the office should approximate the degree of respect women and men *should be* demanding and bestowing in every environment, whether that is on the street, at work, in a bar, seen on television, heard on the radio, or anywhere else. Feminists cannot place the responsibility solely upon men to behave like gentlemen in the office if feminists are not going to insist upon it anywhere else, and women should not be able to turn every instance of tactlessness or misjudgment into a legally actionable offense.

While manners have always been subject to variation depending upon context—that is, people relax their manners in more casual settings—never has there been such a wide disconnect between what is acceptable among the general public and what is allowable in the workplace. When grown men and women have only vague clues about what they should or should not say and do, when employers happily spend thousands of dollars on lawyers and consultants just to instruct employees not only *how to* behave like decent human beings, but to introduce them to the novel idea that *they need to* behave like decent human beings, when thousands of man- (or woman-) hours of unproductive employee time are spent in an effort to protect companies from harassment liability, it should strike any sane person that something is bizarrely wrong.

Thus, while feminists are justifiably concerned about improper conduct in the workplace, they have basically missed the target. Men and women have lost all general and common understanding of good manners. They have been released by our culture from the need to respect the privacy and sensitivity of other people both physically and psychologically. Among the general populace, there is no longer any social pressure upon people to consider the feelings and sensibilities of others in governing their own language and conduct, and there is no longer any sense of reserve between men and women. Under this regime, where society has been allowed to jettison a common language of etiquette, workplace rules have simply become a repressive device, rather than a true shaping of attitudes and behavior. And when women do not generally behave as though they have some personal dignity with respect to their language, their dress, and their conduct; when women do not universally insist upon some measure of decency in every context, it really does not matter what happens in the office. No amount of liability will earn women respect if that respect relies upon a set of stilted, artificial rules grafted onto the business world that have no bearing on behavior anywhere else.

Individual women (and men) who both demonstrate and expressly demand appropriate manners in every instance are much more likely to earn it. If feminists truly seek respect for women, they have to take the position that the unseemly and offensive treatment and discussion of issues related to sexuality that have become so prevalent throughout our culture is socially and politically unacceptable for both men and women in a polite society. And while these things cannot be completely eliminated in our society, crude language and conduct can certainly be relegated to the cultural nether regions they so richly merit, and which they once inhabited.

Of course, modern feminism does not seem as much interested in resolving the challenge of harassment by creating a cultural norm of mutual respect as in gaining a political advantage. Feminism is perfectly happy to extinguish a culturally defined etiquette and to replace it with a whimsically rigid set of legal standards that leaves men mystified as to what is acceptable behavior. Men always risk losing unless they self-censor all of their conduct. It is an insidious sort of oppression in which even innocent comments and a natural desire for collegiality can be filled with risk. And incidentally, while feminists complain about how young men are more likely than young women to receive mentoring in large business firms, they fail to appreciate that they have contributed to this problem through the hyper-promotion of harassment. When older senior management, which is still most often male, can inadvertently expose themselves and their companies to liability when mentoring female underlings, companies can hardly be blamed for exercising a surplus of caution.

Today, a man can get himself fired and his employer sued for telling a woman subordinate that the dress she is wearing is very pretty—but only if she decides to find that comment offensive or filled with suggestive or coercive overtones. Yet, as pointed out in Chapter Seven, feminists are adamant that a middle-aged boss is not guilty of sexual harassment if a young intern who gives him sexual favors is happy to oblige. In the feminist world, it is a feminist's world; reality is a subjective matter—but only for women. It is a world in which, if one sided with Anita Hill, Clarence Thomas is guilty of harassment *even though Ms. Hill did not indicate in any way to him that she found his comments offensive*. Thus, harassment is not about conduct *per se*, but about what a woman *might be* thinking.

This subjective world is one feminists heavily rely upon, notwithstanding the fact that perception is rarely an adequate substitute for the truth. But feminists understand that perception can be more critical in making political impact than hard facts. And nowhere is the issue of feminist subjective perception more blatantly political than in the case of the infamous "glass ceiling," that level beyond which all men have, theoretically, tacitly agreed to keep women underneath.

Much has been made of the glass ceiling, and women are forever being challenged by the contention that they are up against a formidable foe in aiming for the top tier of management and power. But when one begins to delve into the underlying reality of the glass ceiling, it becomes clear that a large portion of the argument relies upon the idea that women are entitled to a certain level of responsibility or authority simply because they have "shown up."

Feminists coined the term "glass ceiling" based upon a single presumption. This presumption is that two to three generations of legal "equality" in the workforce should necessarily have produced the outcome that women would hold a percentage of all political and corporate leadership positions in America roughly equal to the percentage of women in the active workforce. In other words, feminists tend to think earning a leadership role is a simple matter of entitlement. The fact that women do not hold these positions of power is attributed entirely to sexism. For example, Susan Faludi, the author of *Backlash*, flatly rejects the notion that women have "arrived" at equality, and she "proves" this contention by citing statistics showing that women are not represented proportionally on Fortune 500 corporate boards, executive rosters, or law firm partnerships.

Like most statistical information employed in the service of scoring political points, nowhere do Susan Faludi or any of the other feminists crying "Sexism!" cite statistics that provide sufficient explanatory information on male/female demographics in business. Yet there are numerous articles comparing the work experience of men and women that *are* quite relevant. For example, feminists think the bald fact that women earn 78 cents for every dollar a man earns proves that the business world is conspiring against women. Yet studies demonstrate that, once you factor out *real* differences in the career paths of men and women, this disparity dwindles down rapidly. These factors include the number of years women, on average, have dedicated to their career goals; the education and training women have earned; the careers women choose to pursue; the number of women who essentially "opt out" of career interests, even partially or temporarily, in favor of focusing on family; and so on. Once these factors are taken into account, the picture changes dramatically: the pay disparity, in real terms, is closer to 98 cents for every dollar. And any and all of these same factors are relevant to the issue of the glass ceiling.

Consequently, feminists are partly correct that the disparity between the numbers of men and women in management is largely due to sex, but not in the way they suppose. The results are not primarily the product of blind prejudice, of one sex working against the other. Instead, it is the very plain reality that adult men and women approach the work environment from different perspectives and, as groups, have widely diverging career experiences. Men quite naturally have stamped particular corporate cultures on American businesses, and this male-dominated culture continues to prevail in the way business is done, notwithstanding the large proportion of women who work. While feminism has tried to alter the business atmosphere, it has done little to alter the traditional business model.

The American workplace operates upon the principle of competition. Salaries generally depend upon one's education and experience, and companies also favor employees who dedicate long hours, successfully engage in risk, show initiative, and assert themselves. Like it or not, these tend to be masculine strengths. Yet it is feminists who have insisted on "equality" in the workplace, feminists who have insisted that women should compete with men on the same terms that men have always worked. And, as discussed previously, this is so regardless of the fact that women tend to have competing interests in family (to which they often yield) and competing motivations. It is hard to escape the irony of the glass ceiling complaint, when, on the one hand, the feminists of the Yale Journal of Law and Feminism (discussed in Chapter Two) proudly assert that women prefer consensus decision-making and operating, yet on the other hand, feminists insist that women are performing just as well as men in the hierarchical and competitive system on which American businesses operate.

No one with any sense seriously doubts that women are as smart and capable as men; feminism hardly needs a quota to prove it. But simply being smart does not—and never has—earned anyone the top jobs in management. Most women who have succeeded in business have done so by mimicking the habits and traits of men who have succeeded. But, for whatever reason, it is a small percentage of women who follow that pattern. While women make up a large percentage of America's workforce, they do not exhibit the same character traits as men, which means that they are simply going to have different work experiences. For example: where are all the women entrepreneurs, the women who have established their own major law firms, the women venture capitalists, and so on? There are some—and they rightly have the success they have earned. But it is a very small percentage. Few women focus their ambitions in that direction, and the ones who do seem to be perfectly capable of succeeding, notwithstanding the glass ceiling.

The fact is, today, even young childless women raised in post-feminist environs are not out scrapping with their male competition for corporate success. In recent years, lists have been frequently published of top new successful businesses. For example, the website Tecnologia21 listed the top 20 internet millionaires for 2008, youngsters all under 30 (the list included 25 individuals, when counting partnerships). How many of them were women? Just one. But she did not do it on her own; she had a male business partner. Entrepreneur.com, in 2005, profiled 23 hot young entrepreneurs (in all fields) who had become multimillionaires before the age of 40. Of the 23, only 4 were women—and, unlike 7 of the men, none of those 4 had started a company on her own. Surely, particularly in the area of the technology, sexism has little or nothing to do with the fact that men, rather than women, succeed. People are not signing up for Facebook in the millions because it was invented by a man instead of a woman. Granted, these stories do not tell us everything, and they certainly do not mention the many women who have succeeded in business without reaching the pinnacles of multi-millionaire-hood. But they are also not meaningless. Women, as the feminists will surely concede, do not measure success in the same way that men do, and that generally includes such things as extrovert risk-taking and amassing tremendous sums of money. This may be a bad thing (or not), but that does not make it less true.

Feminism cannot simply blame the educational establishments for sexism, either: where are the successful entrepreneurs coming out of Bryn Mawr, Wellesley, and Smith? The fact is, women overwhelmingly choose college majors that do not translate directly into marketability or, more accurately, highly compensated marketability. While women are earning more degrees than men, they are earning them primarily in liberal arts disciplines, rather than in subjects like computer science, engineering or other professional disciplines which are specifically market-oriented, have higher starting salaries than non-technical, non-professional occupations, and which provide more employment opportunities and upward mobility in today's job market. Women make up over half of all college graduates, but are earning only about 25% of the degrees in science-related fields—that is, fields with the high salaries and available job opportunities.

Two generations after they have entered the workforce, women should not expect to run American's companies simply because they have put in the time. While one can quite rationally argue that women bring unique perspectives to corporate leadership, that those perspectives can enhance the performance of companies, and that therefore women should be given more management opportunities, that is not the argument that feminism has been making. Instead, feminists are still intent on putting women on the same playing field as men, and generally under the same rules of play. As a result, feminist expectations about management demographics—that is, that women should be holding as many CEO posts or corporate board memberships as men—are tremendously unrealistic, especially when one considers that most companies and boards are run by men and women in their 50s and 60s. For women to have proportionate representation in top management today would necessarily mean that the first generation of working women would have slogged their way up the corporate ladder even more competitively and successfully than their male counterparts. And that simply did not happen.

It may be quite understandable that feminists do not like the face of corporate America, but there is nothing preventing women from creating their own brand of corporate personality, or creating new structures that they believe more accurately reflect a society focused on women and their ability to contribute to the economy. To a certain extent, some women have been doing that, especially through home-based businesses. But rather than rolling up their sleeves and getting to work, feminist groups are instead pushing ideas like "pay parity" and "comparative worth," which are simply shorthand phrases for assigning arbitrary and increased salaries to traditionally female occupations (such as teaching and social services) to make up for statistical disparities in pay and position between men and women. Quite apart from the fact that a job is only worth what someone is willing to pay someone else to do, it is clear that fudging the numbers does not help women to establish equality. In fact, it proves the opposite: it proves that women are unwilling or incapable of competing in the same job market as men.

Sexism certainly exists, but it is not so rampant that women can hang their hats on that explanation forever. Moreover, whining and complaining may lead to appeasement (and it often has), but rarely does it lead to *actual fairness*. Women who succeed do so regardless of obstacles, and the reality is that the obstacles that exist today are negligible and easily overcome compared to what women faced even 30 years ago. While it is important for blatant and offensive discrimination to be redressed, it is silly for women to allow concepts like the glass ceiling to handicap them—or worse, excuse them. This is not to say that women have no new frontiers to conquer, but griping is unproductive; it is time simply to persevere. After all, if women were consistently and regularly matching or outperforming their male counterparts for 80 cents on the dollar, the reality would be that every employer in America would be firing men and hiring and promoting women. American companies are not shrugging off a 20% margin just because they are run by chauvinistic numbskulls.

Most women encounter and experience some bias, whether it is because they are women, they are not as good-looking as someone else, they have a funny name, they have bad taste in footwear, or what-have-you. It is easy, and quite valid, to claim that it is *not fair* that the world is not operated strictly as a meritocracy. But so what? Working smarter and striving to achieve is not about women besting men; it is about meeting individual potential, exceeding expectations, and improving. Employers who do not recognize and reward performance are not doing themselves any favors. No one is forcing women, particularly women in the management fast-track, to stay where they are. If women truly believe their bosses and employers are shortchanging them, they need to show a little spine by backing up that belief with action: walk out the door and get a more lucrative or higher position, demand a raise, or pursue a promotion by outperforming the competition. If women want to compete with men on the same playing field, they need to adopt the same attitudes to business as men. And if this is *not* what women want, they need to be creating their own corporate culture that more accurately reflects feminine values.

It is hard to tolerate feminism's lament that women are being discriminated against if women are simply clinging helplessly to their jobs, only to grumble privately about how they are under-appreciated. *Of course* employees are under-appreciated; one rarely hears of bosses ever calling an employee into the office to say, "Gosh, you are worth so much more than we pay you. Here's a raise." Companies are having a hard enough time staying in business and making profits; they do not spend their time worrying about whether an employee's bruised feelings need coddling. Employers are always going to pay less for the performance of a job than the net income that job ultimately provides to the employer. (Unless, of course, the employer is an arm of government or a U.S. automaker, in which case it will pay whatever the union demands until the government runs into debt or the company is driven into bankruptcy, at which time the employer will ask that the U.S. taxpayer continue to fund union benefits.) Just as anyone with sense will buy a television from someone who sells it $100 cheaper than his competitor, an employer would rather pay less to get a job done than pay more. To the extent that women are making significantly less than their male counterparts or less than an employer derives from their performance, it is high time women stood up for themselves, individually, and shouldered the responsibility to narrow that gap and reap a better bargain. That is the nature of a market economy. That is the nature of competition.

Too often, women simply resent the bare fact of pay disparity, then gripe to their feminist allies about how much more they are worth while they sit back, safely ensconced behind a wall of anonymity, as a feminist organization complains to a Senate committee or executive branch commission. Not only is it spineless, it is amazingly ineffective. Unless women, like men, are willing to stand up for themselves and assert any real or perceived disparities in the particular, to actually demonstrate the independence and strength they say they want and that they have earned, they are likely to get precisely what they have asked for: nothing.

SECTION SIX: THE MORAL LANDSCAPE

Chapter Eighteen: From Seeking Liberation to Demanding Dependence in Less Than Two Generations

Some women now enjoy the right to abortion—but not the 44 million women, from the indigent to the military work force, who depend on the federal government for their medical care.

. . .

The backlash line blames the women's movement for the "feminization of poverty"—while the backlash's own instigators in Washington pushed through the budget cuts that helped impoverish millions of women, fought pay equity proposals, and undermined equal opportunity laws. The backlash line claims the women's movement cares nothing for children's rights— while its own representatives in the capital and state legislatures have blocked one bill after another to improve child care, slashed billions of dollars in federal aid for children, and relaxed state licensing standards for day care centers. The backlash line accuses the women's movement of creating a generation of unhappy single and childless women—but its purveyors in the media are the ones guilty of making single and childless women feel like circus freaks.

To blame feminism for women's "lesser life" is to miss entirely the point of feminism, which is to win women a wider range of experience. . . .

The meaning of the word "feminist" has not really changed since it first appeared in . . . 1895, describing a woman who "has in her the capacity of fighting her way back to independence." . . . It asks that women be free to define themselves—instead of having their identity defined for them, time and again, by their culture and their men."

--Susan Faludi

Did Ms. Faludi read what she was writing? In this short passage, one learns that feminists are not responsible for the policies that led to impoverishing women . . . because Congress could have rescued these women by providing better welfare benefits. Women are only capable of caring for their own children . . . when government strengthens day-care legislation and forces taxpayers to support them. Women cannot be independent . . . unless they can reliably depend upon government entitlements. Rights are not rights . . . unless the government pays for the ability to exercise them. And women are not free to define themselves until the media defines them how they want to be defined. This is from the introduction to the book *Backlash*. If this is the face of feminism, it is no wonder radical feminists scorn the use of reason.

To get to the bottom of the complaint: who, exactly, is preventing women from defining themselves today? The social conditions that affect women have changed a great deal in the last century, and even more acutely in the last few decades. Almost all of those changes have been in the direction that the feminist movement has advocated, everything from Title IX funding in women's college sports to finding a constitutional right to abortion. Women have unprecedented opportunities before them, unprecedented choices, unprecedented freedom. But despite these changes, the feminists seem to have gathered up even more injustices to gripe about than they did half a century ago. Modern feminism has changed the rules of the game, from a quest for liberation into a pathetic demand for salvation. If women's "freedom to define themselves" is so dependent upon what other people do, it is a very peculiar brand of freedom, indeed.

The truth is that feminists have been defining women day in and day out for the last three decades. As a matter of fact, that seems to be what many feminists spend most of their time trying to do. But they have neither arrived at a consistent answer, nor an answer they find satisfactory. More importantly, nothing they have proposed has made any headway in making women something other than what they are.

This, ultimately, is the error that leads modern feminists to encounter the problems they have encountered: the inability to discern what women are because they are too busy trying to redefine what they would like women to be. And nowhere is this more true than with respect to the three social issues that have become the engine that drives the modern feminist movement today: casual sexual experimentation, the normalization of homosexuality, and the push for an unfettered right to abortion.

Though the relationship may not be entirely apparent at first, there is a very close relationship between casual sex, abortion, and homosexuality: all attempt to erase or deny the procreative element from sexual intercourse. And though the feminists do not readily concede or even recognize this fact, these three prongs of feminist policy lead to a very disturbing portrait of what they see as the future of modern American womanhood, not to mention humanity. Placing these ideas at the core of its movement is what has made modern feminism sexless. Together, they attempt to erase the reality of what it means to be female. Together, they try to conceptualize sex as something other than— *anything* other than—the means of human procreation, and try to portray women as having some identity that is isolated or divorced from sexuality. This is a feminism that tries to neuter women, a feminism that views the maternal role and character of women as something to be diminished, avoided, shunned, or quashed. And while women do not need to become mothers in order to be women, no woman can be true who denies, denigrates, or tries to eliminate the mortal obligation of what it means to be female.

What is more, casual sex, abortion, and homosexuality all contribute significantly toward establishing a culture of asexuality and narcissism. The phrase "culture of asexuality" may sound odd, since "sex" is everywhere: on television, in books, magazines, movies, and all over the internet. However, most of the sex that is being force-fed to American society completely discounts its procreative aspects, or more disturbingly, views it as a "side effect" to sex's more immediate and superficial appeal. Thus, because "sex" is, by definition, the means by which life recreates itself, most of what people talk about is not sex at all, but merely intercourse-related sexual activities. This may be an unattractive, cumbersome, and unimaginative phrase to describe what is being discussed, but it seems to have taken on so many forms that one is at a loss for how otherwise to describe it. And while modern feminists may object to the oversexed world daily on display—or, at least, certain aspects of it—the fact is that their positions contribute to this debasement of sex, and the debasement of women.

The repeated thrumming of the theme that women should "control their own reproduction" is, consequently, also a figurative form of male castration. And while most women likely do not see it this way, the theme, for modern feminists, is probably intentional. Claiming the right to remove from men any control over the ability to engender offspring essentially renders men impotent. The undermining of a man's basic instinctual drive to perpetuate his life, and the complacency with which modern feminists assert for women (married or not) a unilateral and unfettered power over whether to bear any offspring, is understandably frustrating to many men. This "right" that the feminists so glibly mouth is, by implication, a rather vicious form of rejecting men.

This section of the book discusses these key social and moral issues—sexual activity unrelated to procreation, homosexuality, and abortion—that modern feminism has sought to (and largely succeeded in) revolutionizing. Through a careful dissection of what modern feminism's motivations are, and how it has gone about advancing this new social ethos, one can see that modern feminism's aims are almost completely divorced from—and diametrically opposed to—advancing the interests of real women.

Chapter Nineteen: There are Times When Sex Really Does Matter

A liberated woman is one who has sex before marriage and a job after.

--Gloria Steinem

It should go without saying, but sex is no small matter in defining the difference between men and women. What is more, there is a purpose to that difference, no matter how much feminists try to negate that difference in particular settings. And that purpose has to do with the fact that, whatever else sexual intercourse is, its principal and defining purpose is that of producing offspring. It is the means by which the human race, as well as virtually every other living thing, perpetuates itself. While there are all sorts of social implications of sex in every culture, the bottom line is the biological one: women and men engage in intercourse in order to create human life. Once you fully understand and appreciate the significance of that basic premise, the depravity of the feminist movement with respect to female sexuality becomes very stark.

While some women clearly do not subscribe to feminist ideas on sex outside of marriage, many women do, at least to a certain degree. American women have been persuaded that this view of sex is simply "modern" or "sophisticated" or "mature," and that the women who went before them were merely poor unfortunates who suffered from a lack of medical technology.

Women who completely adopt this mindset become convinced that their own sexuality is primarily a plaything. But it most assuredly is not. Women's bodies and their capacity to bring a new life into being are precious and remarkable. What is more, the modern view quite unfoundedly assumes that women are somehow capable of managing their new bio-technological "tools" more wisely than their forebears dealt with nature.

It is not entirely clear why, but at some point, feminists decided that women could not be liberated unless and until society eliminated what they dubbed the "double standard": if men could sleep around before marriage and not be socially penalized, then women could and should do the same. As noted previously, this attitude coupled with the advent of the Pill gave birth to the sexual revolution: socially, sexual intercourse was no longer reserved for married couples, but was promoted as a national pastime. Women could be as detached and cavalier about sexual encounters as men. Right.

The strange thing is that so many women bought into and continue to buy into this ridiculous ambition. Yet there really is no rational basis for why feminists made "sexual freedom" part and parcel to the well-being and economic "liberation" of women. With amazing swiftness, they adopted with a religious fervor the idea that women could easily overcome biological reality, and were therefore released from social restrictions on widespread extramarital sex. But the consequences were predictable. This is not to say that some women are not pleased to live a less restrictive lifestyle. The point is that, *as a tenet within the women's movement*, its adoption has quite clearly not made women, as a group, better off or more independent. But by freeing men from many of the restrictions and rules that used to govern their sexual behavior, it has allowed men to be supremely independent. As mentioned previously, the "feminization" of sex did more to liberate men from the social straightjacket of a "patriarchal" culture than it did women.

Casual sex may seem like a nifty idea and a heck of a lot of fun, but it is only in the feminists' intellectually constructed, and erroneously conceived, world that it has no consequences—either emotional or physical. Unfortunately, for the women who bought into feminism's embrace of sex outside of marriage, no amount of intellectualizing can or does erase the fact that women carry and bear children. Because feminists were so eager to discard what they characterized as oppressive moral rules that imposed unpleasant social consequences, they failed to appreciate that the laws of nature might impose even harsher rules and more material consequences than "prudish" social mores.

But feminists urged all of America to shake off their consciences, consign middle-class mores to the trashcan, and embrace "sexual freedom." So women cast off the tyranny of morality for the tyranny of biology or, at the very least, for an uneasy servitude to medical science. Quite naturally, and as discussed in greater detail in Section 3, with more sexual activity outside of marriage, more women became pregnant, more women began to have children out of wedlock, and more women found themselves alone and economically disadvantaged. The feminist response was typical, and typically wrong-headed: America's young women need more sex education, more contraception, and legalized abortion (funded, of course, by tax dollars). As NOW's website confirms, these stances have become hallmarks of the feminist platform. Instead of protecting themselves with virtue, women now gird themselves with the armor of cumbersome birth control, soul-destroying abortion, and emotional insecurity. To the dismay of many women now saddled with the economic burden of raising their illegitimate children with no help, this has not been a particularly welcome and beneficial trade-off.

One cannot help but ponder: suppose a group of disgruntled and chauvinistic men had proposed, 50 years ago, that: 1) women should freely engage in sexual intercourse with a wide variety of men without regard to marital commitment; 2) women should simply and zealously employ birth control methods to avoid the consequences of their loose sexual conduct; and 3) if any women became pregnant despite their precautions (or, more likely, by failing to faithfully exercise sufficient precautions), they could easily and carelessly abort their unborn children, rather than rely upon the old shotgun method of roping men into observing the convention of marriage for the sake of their honor and offspring. And, of course, let us not ignore the ultimate Option 4: if women decided to have their children anyway, well, it has been nice knowing you: good-bye and good luck.

The reaction from women, including women who considered themselves feminists, would have been outrage at such a callous, cold-hearted, and demeaning view of both sexual intercourse and women. Yet this is precisely the scheme modern feminists have happily signed on to. In giddier moments, one can imagine groups of men, sitting in their exclusive gentlemen's clubs in the 60's and 70's, lighting up cigars and patting themselves on the back for concocting this ingenious scheme to liberate themselves from the confines of marriage and responsibility. As alluded to previously, this scheme has bestowed upon men a species of moral and economic freedom they could scarcely have imagined.

Unfortunately, many women who adopted the "free sex" mentality quickly realized that it did not free them at all—at least, it did not free them from reality, however much it may have freed them from their own consciences. It did not make men respect them, or motivate men to treat women as equals. And how could it? The irony was that in removing the central focus of sex away from procreation—that is, *removing from sex all its gravity*—the feminists helped to marginalize women not only as a social force, but, in many cases, as individuals. When sex has no purpose, women cannot avoid, to some extent, becoming seen by men primarily as sex objects, rather than the caretakers and nurturers of the human race overall and the next generation of humans in particular. And this is precisely the social change that emerged: the sexual revolution did not inspire men to regard women as equals, but, in some sense, to place them on an even lower rung. The social tradition by which decent men were expected to demonstrate a sense of honor with respect to all women has virtually disappeared.

Without procreation as a moderating or governing influence in the act of intercourse, sex no longer has *any* significant function, let alone a deeper emotional component. Men are free to regard sex with women as simply one more recreational outlet, like softball and poker night. The sexual revolution did little to liberate women as a group, because it failed to liberate women individually. In effect, women simply traded in their virtue for a more committed relationship to their pharmacists and gynecologists—and a less committed relationship to the men in their lives. Birth control and abortion, essential once one accepts the casual sex mentality, finally allowed feminists to reinvent womanhood. But as what?

As discussed in detail previously, despite their incessant blather about "controlling" reproduction, feminists seem not to realize that procreation is simply unavoidable in a world in which sexual intercourse is taking place with indiscriminate frequency. And when people demonstrate an unwillingness to exercise control over their sexual appetites, it is not the human race that is in danger of extinction, it is human dignity. Moreover, it is a dignity that was kept vital by the existence of the very social structures—ethical mores, marriage, and family—that feminists derided as "too limiting" for women.

The speed with which casual sex became adopted as a social norm was hardly surprising. By casting the issue as if it embodied the virtue of "liberation," rather than the vice of licentiousness, women found a way to rationalize away any of their moral misgivings. Feminists rode high on the heady feeling that they could advance any idea through activism, never suspecting that the motivations that prompted society to follow its lead on "free sex" were not due to the merits of the idea, but because it appealed to people's baser instincts. Yet feminism took this cue to heart, and has since adopted the belief that any idea, no matter how unsupportable or irrational, can be advanced through activism, and that the rest of the world will simply and easily reshape itself to accommodate their caprice. With dumbfounding frequency, the feminist movement persists in thinking that a new reality can be created simply by wishing it into being.

Feminists, rather than seeing all sides of sexual intercourse as part of one organic act with an actual purpose, tried to characterize it as a multi-faceted activity. Several generations of women have now grown up under the feminist-inspired impression that they can easily and neatly divide their sexual lives up into discrete segments. In order to fully "liberate" themselves from the shackles of a male-dominated culture, they can compartmentalize their sexual activities into sex for experimentation, sex for recreation, sex for personal satisfaction, sex for emotional expression, sex for commitment, and, last and apparently least, sex for procreation. But despite this handy conceptualization, the ability to segregate their emotions has been, for the most part, elusive for women; the specter of procreation always and necessarily remains. While college-educated professional women with high-powered careers like to act the sophisticate with regard to sex, the real world is not so neat. In the end, while one cannot dispute the pleasurable and emotional aspects of sex, it is impossible to divorce it from procreation.

But this has not, unfortunately, stopped many young women from falling into the trap created by that conceptualization. Many young women today, growing up in a culture heavily influenced by feminist ideas about casual sex and too often raised without any moral guidance with regard to sex, enter into sexual relationships in the naïve faith that their own biological functions are easily understood and effortlessly manipulated. Young women become sexually active simply because they feel like it. They are not encouraged to ask themselves whether they would like to bear the child of the boy with whom they are sleeping (much less whether the boy would care to have a child), as though that issue is irrelevant. These youngsters barely even realize that having sex is a choice at all. Instead, they treat sexual activity as if it were a normal and expected thing to jump into whenever they feel they are "ready," as though they are talking about learning to drive a car.

As stated previously, making sex less meaningful has made women *less* significant, as well. Women, as mere sexual partners, have become fungible commodities, rather than lifelong partners and companions. And while yesteryear's puritanical condemnation of loose women may have been overly harsh, moral rules pertaining to abstinence before marriage were not simply arbitrary. Such rules had a tremendously pragmatic aspect in helping to ensure that children were brought up by committed couples who publicly and purposefully expressed their commitment to a family prior to creating one. Ironically, today, by embracing sex as something other than a means of creating new life, pregnancy is treated as though it is some sort of anomaly, and children as something less than human.

It is hard to imagine a more pointed example of this than President Barack Obama's defense of his stance on sex education in regard to sexually transmitted diseases (specifically, HIV and AIDS) during his 2008 campaign. Discussing the subject, he stated:

> So, when it comes to—when it comes specifically to HIV/AIDS, the most important prevention is education, which should include— which should include abstinence only—should include abstinence education and teaching that children—teaching children, you know, that sex is not something casual. But it should also include—it should also include other, you know, information about contraception because, look, I've got two daughters—9 years old and 6 years old. I'm going to teach them first of all about values and morals, but if they make a mistake, I don't want them punished with a baby. I don't want them punished with an STD at the age of 16.

When then-Senator Obama received tremendous criticism from his detractors for his injudicious use of the word "punished," his defenders rushed to his aid, trying to explain that, within the context of his discussion, he did not state that pregnancy was a "punishment." But they missed the point. True, Barack Obama was not making an assertion that pregnancy was a "punishment" as a general matter. But his choice of language even within the context of the discussion is revealing about the modern mindset regarding sex—and, particularly, the mindset regarding sex that is endorsed by feminism.

Barack Obama's choice of words signaled his glib acceptance of the notion that engaging in sex is a normal and expected teenage behavior. If one is teaching about extramarital sex as a moral matter, it is most assuredly not a "mistake," rather, it is an affirmative wrong. And the consequence of becoming pregnant or contracting an STD may be an unwanted consequence, but it is a relatively common and predictable consequence of sexual intercourse, whether or not one uses birth control. In fact, the very discussion of HIV and AIDs should give any rational person pause in contemplating the tenor of sex education, particularly when discussing one's daughters.

But most significantly, Barack Obama's choice of words reveals a mindset that treats pregnancy as a by-product of sex, or even less; his flimsy language about being "punished" with a baby signals his implicit acceptance, without question, that getting pregnant is *almost never the actual purpose of sex*. We have generations of individuals and an entire culture in which the truth about sex is completely shrouded by this fiction, and our culture embraces this fiction because it is ultimately more alluring than reality. We can pretend that, because sex is just a meaningless recreational activity, our responsibilities are just as casually undertaken as the sex. In the end, the real depravity of Barack Obama's statement is this: if he actually believes that sex is a moral question and that engaging in casual sex is a "mistake," then what he needs to teach his daughters, first and foremost, is that *sex is about having babies*.

This position is not even fundamentally moral; it is simply truthful. Unless one trumpets that basic fact, then teaching youths about the seriousness of sex or even about contraception and STDs is simply a waste of time. They will—quite understandably—continue to hop in the sack according to their whims, and they (and the rest of society) will ultimately pay the price in terms of the medical costs of STDs and abortions, the emotional costs of abortion and unwed parenthood, the welfare and social costs of single motherhood, and the social and criminal costs of parentless children.

In contrast to this bleak and troubled portrait of a casual sex culture and where that leads, the old-fashioned model of moral straightness is refreshingly simple and straightforward. Women who firmly and squarely draw the line at marriage have a distinct advantage: they never need to question their own value, nor question the motivations of the men with whom they have a relationship. Women who stand upon the principle that sex is primarily about having children, and that having children is only appropriate or desirable within the context of a stable and committed marriage, are doing nothing more nor less than accepting the reality of their sex and of society. That position is one of strength, not of weakness. The social mores which favored abstinence operated quite successfully under this truism, and it is silly for feminists today to claim that medical science has somehow overshadowed this reality. This is not to say that everyone must be a puritan, or that society must condemn women who do not adhere to this standard. But it does mean that the feminists' desperate grip on the slogan of "reproductive control" is hardly a liberating creed. By waving the banner of "reproductive control," all they are really saying is that they want to be able to have sex without any responsibility, or, more plainly, that they resent the fact that women are, in fact, women.

Reducing sex to a recreational activity has not only diminished women, it has had an unappealing flip side, as well: it has made men much less than they can be, and much less than our society needs them to be. Men certainly are not complaining about the sexual "liberation" of women, and no wonder. How on earth did feminists ever imagine that giving men virtually unfettered access to sex unencumbered by commitment would somehow earn women the "respect" as equals that men had previously withheld? When women of "virtue" possessed the natural authority that virtue bestows, men, as a general rule, were persistently forced to observe the social niceties required of gentlemen, lest they lose the company of all respectable women, and lest they lose all hope of making a good marriage. And certainly married men, tied as they once were to lifelong marriage (or, at the very least, lifelong financial support of their wives and children), were unlikely to seriously stray since the costs both socially and economically of leaving their wives and children were grave.

By abetting men in avoiding the need to confront any procreative consequences of their sexual (mis)conduct, and by claiming to themselves an exclusive right to control reproduction, feminists have completely ceded the field to an utterly chauvinistic social structure. The sexual revolution has not given feminists a lever to strengthen and raise the stature of women with respect to men. On the contrary, the sexual revolution has filled our society with even fewer men who have moral fortitude and a sense of social responsibility than generations past. It has diminished everyone.

In the modern world, men need not meet any social standard of respectability with regard to women, and rarely face social criticism or judgment at all with respect to licentious sexual behavior. On the contrary, even feminists acknowledge that men are expected to get what they can get, so long as women reserve the power to say "No." All women are fair game, and, what is more, that game is rarely for "keeps." Men do not have to compete with one another to obtain the "prize" of a woman they admire, desire, or love; instead, they can have any number of women for varying lengths of time, then they can simply move on or trade off with other men when the women they are with lose their luster, their youth, or their appeal, particularly when those women start to pressure them into giving them things like a wedding band or children. Under the modern regime, there is no requirement at all for men to respect or value women, either collectively or individually. Rather, men are utterly free to be cavalier and cruel, and for callous behavior they pay no social penalty whatsoever.

Further, the "sexual revolution" has done virtually nothing to "empower" women as a group. The "freedom" to sleep around may provide women with transient sexual satisfaction, but it has no claim to giving women more power politically, socially, emotionally, or economically, and it certainly has failed utterly in elevating the stature of women in regard to men. As a matter of fact, it has shifted women in the other direction, and in critically important ways. By surrendering the high ground on sex—the high ground being that sex is not about physical self-gratification, but about respecting and appreciating one's body, and believing that sex is irrefutably attached to procreation—women have in fact made themselves more dependent than ever. Many of the women who have fallen prey to the feminists' touted wonders of the sexual revolution have found themselves not independently strong, standing on their own two feet and out conquering a man's world.

Instead, they have watched their once-glowing opportunities and dreams for a good education, a promising career, and a strong marriage and family life limited or narrowed by the responsibilities of single motherhood, or their physical and mental strength and confidence stunted by the shame and trauma caused by a youthfully foolish and fear-induced abortion. Other women who have avoided pregnancy yet embraced this lifestyle have found that it is not without its own problems. Quite apart from the worries and fear of pregnancy and STDs, they often find out that having regular sex is not a very good surrogate for marriage. After a few years, the "freedom" of having independent bank accounts, credit cards, and exotic holidays loses some of its luster. Not surprisingly, the thought of being able to enjoy the "mundane" comforts of raising their own much-loved children and going to bed with a man who promises to be around in the morning begins to have great appeal.

Even women who reject the feminist message about the delights of irresponsible sexual activity are handicapped by the new ethic. Men they meet and women they know apply more pressure than ever upon them to willingly subject their bodies (and emotional stability) to the caprice of their baser natural instincts, rather than to their highest ideals and aspirations. Men have come to expect women to be "mature" about sex, by which they mean that women should feel perfectly comfortable with the idea that sex is simply an amusement. Understandably, men have been more than happy to advance that feminist message to prospective bed-partners, and more than happy to employ the feminist rationalization that any other behavior is simply outmoded.

While women who are strong in adhering to their own standards are not swayed by this pretext, their futures, too, are dimmed by the modern sexual orthodoxy. Men who are in all other respects decent have become so comfortable with the (false) idea that birth control handily and easily compensates for any other considerations that they cannot fathom what might compel a woman to reserve her body for something a little more profound than a semi-serious mostly monogamous boyfriend-girlfriend relationship.   Sexual morality is seen not within the context of what it says about strength of character or self-respect, but is frequently treated like a religious or fundamentalist relic that is just short of lunacy.   This attitude in men, unfortunately, is understandable, since men do not belong to the sex that ultimately must bear responsibility for carelessness—at least, not since the feminists conveniently and recklessly convinced them that men are not allowed to have any reproductive control (and therefore reproductive responsibility) at all.   Thus, women who refuse to succumb to the pressures of modern social mores may find that more than a few men are quite mystified by their stance on sex, and many of these men will simply vanish from the field of prospects.   After all, if there are plenty of "respectable" women who have no qualms about sex outside of marriage, then there hardly seems to be any reason for men to pursue women who *do* have qualms.

And while it is true that most of these men and women will ultimately find someone to marry and with whom to have a family despite the social handicaps of working at cross purposes, the result is sad, nonetheless.   We have a society in which the standards of sexual behavior are emotionally and physically risky to women and which encourage male irresponsibility—and not merely irresponsibility with respect to the consequences of sex, but irresponsibility in terms of providing the emotional support of love and constancy.   Those women who choose to avoid these risks in favor of exercising actual control of their physiological and emotional well-being are now not even bestowed the respect that at one time was their due, and their prospects for marriage are accordingly narrowed by the reality that men no longer need to contemplate marriage in order to satisfy their natural sexual urgings on a regular basis.

While this may sound somewhat silly when stated explicitly, it has a real and material social impact. The fact is, men, like women, do crave love, emotional stability, and the continuity and support that may be provided by a spouse and children. But, unlike women, men are not nearly as handicapped by age; they can comfortably put off settling down until well into middle age, and still enjoy the prospect of having a youthful wife and family. Thus, with ready access to sexual pleasure unaccompanied by any obligations or social stigma whatsoever, young men have been handed a tremendous capacity to remain emotionally immature for an extended length of time. They often proceed well into their thirties, or beyond, without ever having to capably manage the responsibilities and burdens that otherwise compel a man to seriously order his priorities, and neither are they forced to confront the sorts of serious emotional and pragmatic dilemmas of family life that focus their minds and attention on matters that might give some deeper meaning or purpose to their lives. In many ways, men are not compelled, for many years, to "grow up" and behave like, well, like *men*, as opposed to perpetual adolescents.

This is not to say that there are not young, single men who exhibit maturity with respect to their relationships to women. But there is little that *requires* them to mature and to confront adult issues with adult perspectives. Ironically, or perhaps not so ironically, the sexual revolution so happily embraced by feminists coddles and promotes the very men the feminists profess to condemn: men who are irresponsible, immature, and chauvinistic, men who are inclined to view women as objects. Of course, the flip-side to this kind of man is one feminists heavily depend upon: this very irresponsibility and immaturity gives the feminists precisely the kind of man who is more than eager to promote female "emancipation" from old sexual taboos, and more than happy to endorse feminist ideas about contraception and abortion.

In a very real way, the men who are abetting feminism's views on sexuality have become less than men, just as feminists have progressed in making women less than women. In the interest of satisfying the fleeting fancies of their own libidos, men who like the idea of free and easy access to sex have failed to appreciate that they are promoting their own emasculation. Quite literally, they are condoning the concept that, however virile they imagine that they are, they are nonetheless impotent in a physical, social, and even legal sense to have any say-so in the begetting of their own offspring. Thus, men are confronted by two inherently contradictory standards: they are denied any rights whatsoever in the decision to bear children, yet at the same time are being told they must shoulder full responsibility for the welfare of those children once they are born, either individually or collectively. But feminists are also blind to the pitfalls of this contradiction: men who have been rendered impotent have a perfectly legitimate claim to having no interest whatsoever in children.

Consequently, the term "sexual revolution" aptly captures the war-like aspects of this cultural shift. The perceived conquering of traditional morals and customs by the dubious wonders of medical science has been embraced wholeheartedly by the feminist movement and accepted rapidly by the rest of society. Only a few reflective souls have had the nerve and presence of mind to question the broader implications of what that has boded for our culture. To date, the primary casualties of this revolution have not been men, whatever feminists may have intended, but children. Children have been recast by feminists as "extras" at best and "inconveniences" at worst. This is part and parcel of applying the modern narcissistic feminist philosophy in which life is solely about defining and serving the self, and not about any responsibilities women should bear in order to create a better society.

However much the feminists might like the idea that they are nominally succeeding in transforming men into something less than they were before, both the men and the women who are complicit in advancing this feminist vision fail to appreciate that this is a mutually destructive strategy. Men and women live in the world together, and they will continue to need to do so. At the very least, they should attempt to do so in a way that appreciates their respective roles in a natural world, and recognize that, just as they were once children (believe it or not), the well-being of all children is most emphatically a matter of critical importance. Children cannot be relegated to the status of a by-product of sex if our culture is to flourish, let alone survive.

Feminism does not see sexual activity as invoking any social responsibility. Instead, it has approached sex from the standpoint that it is solely another "right" to which all women are entitled, like the right to speak or the right to vote. They have wholeheartedly thrown their weight into retraining society not only into thinking that this is a valid approach, but that it is a healthy one. Thanks to feminists and the sexual revolution, sex is no longer a natural or sacred act, it is a political one. Casual sex is an implicit endorsement of the idea that nature has it all wrong, and we know better.

The personal is the political, indeed.

Chapter Twenty: Homosexuality—the the Ultimate Misogyny

The simple fact is that every woman must be willing to be identified as a lesbian to be fully feminist.

--Sheila Cronan

Gay Liberation? I ain't against it, it's just that there's nothing in it for me.

--Bette Davis

The political character of sex, and the rejection of women's sexual attributes, is nowhere clearer than in the modern feminists' promotion of homosexuality and, further, in the feminists' support of the highly pressing issue of normalizing homosexual "marriage."

It must be reiterated here that it is a mystery, in a rational sense, why the feminists should tie their tail to the advancement of homosexuality in general, and homosexual "marriage" in particular. It should be self-evident that the only purpose for the existence of a feminist movement *per se* is to somehow recognize the distinct role of women, and to use the movement to advance ideas that have something particular to do with the roles and concerns of women. Why then homosexuality? Clearly, there is nothing about homosexuality that has any particular meaningfulness for women as distinct from men. However much the feminists claim that their sympathies are based upon supporting other "victims" of cultural oppression, one suspects the real connection is more disturbing. The significant connection between feminism and homosexuality is that the latter also advances the destruction of marriage and of the family, and advances the politicization of sex that fits within the peculiar context of the feminist agenda.

Having reduced the sexual act to nothing more than a pastime, and completely discounted and undermined the procreative purpose of sex, the feminists can now advance homosexuality as no different than heterosexuality, and human relationships as nothing beyond a quest for self-serving companionship and sexual satisfaction. Again, it is striking how utterly disturbing this vision of womanhood is. The feminists have essentially idealized the notion that fully realized womanhood is a state that is, quite literally, "liberated" from the fact of being a woman at all. And this is why that attitude is misogynistic: the active opposition to the natural functions of their own bodies is a graphic demonstration of their contempt for, and rejection of, actual womanhood in favor of some intellectualized version of womanhood that has no biological component.

Consistent with this view, it is not difficult to conjecture that the next logical frontiers for this movement are the legitimization of, for example, incest and prostitution. The fact is, if sex is unrelated to procreation by the handy devices of birth-control and abortion, and marriage is merely a temporary legal status convened for the purposes of economic or social partnership accompanied by self-serving pleasure, social taboos against virtually any sexual perversion, including incest, simply disappears. Similarly, prostitution merely becomes an economic transaction. If one wholly accepts the feminist insistence on the autonomy of women to do what they want with their own bodies, the inevitability of legitimizing prostitution becomes a no-brainer.

Accordingly, it makes perfect sense for the feminists to advance homosexuality as part of the feminist agenda. Homosexuality is completely consistent with the feminist use of the "rights" dialectic, and its peculiar insistence upon the concept that woman have the right to do with their bodies what they want. If women's bodies are simply the possession of the women who inhabit them, then, the argument goes, women have the right to do whatever they want to those bodies, and society's interests are necessarily inferior.

But this assertion of "rights" is frequently cast in a way that undermines a true understanding of rights, and this is so with respect to the "right" to marry being asserted by homosexuals and promoted by the feminist movement. Put simply, a "right" is merely a freedom to engage in an activity in which the government may not, without grave public interests, interfere. Thus, marriage is not a "right" at all. Instead, marriage is, to a large extent, a privilege that is, if not actually bestowed by government, then, to a significant degree, endowed by government recognition. And that is exactly where the homosexual marriage debate rages. It should strike anyone as significant that the realm in which the battle is being fought is whether the law should affirmatively recognize and validate homosexual unions, not whether the law should refrain from interfering in homosexual relationships. In the marriage question, homosexual couples are asking for positive and favorable government intervention.

Homosexuals already have the right to engage in homosexual activity; that is a "right" as the term is properly understood. And even ardent Christians who view homosexuality as immoral have generally conceded that advocating the illegality of homosexual activity is a futile crusade. But one does not simply "marry" on one's own. Marriage is, and always has been, a public act, and a public status; it is most assuredly not a "private" affair. In fact, one cannot obtain government recognition of marriage without meeting government-defined criteria; whole bodies of law and whole court systems have been developed to handle the issues of marriage and the resultant family, as well as their dissolution. Thus, it is a falsehood to characterize the matter as one of personal civil liberty as opposed to public policy. What the feminists and homosexual community are seeking is not freedom, but public approval, and their insistence upon the "rights" terminology is resolutely aimed at obscuring the fact that this is not a question of rights at all.

This is not to say that that settles the matter. As such things go, homosexual marriage is a matter of legal policy, and legislated legal policy at that; only time will tell which cultural value prevails. And in point of fact, this reliance upon the law as the ultimate arbiter of cultural values is in many ways the *modus operandi* of the feminist movement, as it seems to be for every leftist movement. In this, as in so many liberal issues, the law, and control of the law, is the only thing that matters. To the feminist mindset, law and government policy are the only relevant expression of social values. All other considerations have no force in the face of the law. Having squarely jettisoned the idea that there is some existing objective or spiritual means of determining the principles that ought to govern individual conduct and social values, laws become, for them, the only expression of public standards, and they imagine that law and government policy serve as an entirely adequate substitute for morality or conscience or duty or charity. To the feminist, if the law does not advocate everything they want, the world is unfair and oppressive, and the law must be changed.

This is also why feminists work so diligently on government funding of their causes. As a political movement, feminism never operates under the principle that, even when something is allegedly important to them, it is their own personal responsibility to shoulder and promote. Rather, the burden must fall on everyone equally, including upon those who are diametrically opposed to the policy thus being advanced. This, ultimately, is why the question is not one of "rights." Those who oppose the law are denied even the right to respectably disagree: they have to support, through funding, ideas that are entirely abhorrent to their principles and consciences.

The investment made by the feminist movement into advancing the policy of homosexual marriage fits this mold. It matters not even an iota to them how many people may feel about homosexuality as a moral or even as a civil matter. Just as in abortion, they do not intend to leave even the remotest margin of wiggle room in the public discourse for opposing sensibilities. In so many ways, *Roe v. Wade*, the 1973 Supreme Court decision that discovered a right to an abortion, is the ultimate feminist victory, not just in terms of subject matter, but in terms of strategy. By making a right to abortion a matter of constitutional interpretation, they bypassed all the messy necessity of winning the issue in the minds of the public, and dramatically eliminated the need to advance the idea through incremental inroads into the minds and consciences of a reluctant and skeptical public—a reluctance and skepticism, incidentally, which persists nearly four decades after the fact.

With homosexual marriage, feminists have sought to use this same strategy, and, to a certain degree, it has worked. Their victories on this issue have relied upon state court decisions, and not upon democratic processes—except as a post-litigation stop-gap measure. Today, the quest to force-feed homosexual marriage to a populace that is clearly (as of the time of this writing) not prepared to accept it is emblematic of this leftist mode of operation. In some ways, this is an admission of weakness, an implicit acknowledgment of the fact that the idea they are promoting lacks, by itself, the requisite appeal or merit sufficient to gain popular acceptance. In this as in so many things, feminists are not convinced of their idea's power to persuade; rather, they are determined to dictate. And even more, they are dead set on dictating to those who most staunchly disagree. It is very much a "shoot first, ask questions later" tactic, and it has been enormously effective.

The battle wages on. It is not enough for homosexuals to be free from job discrimination or to be free from legal proscription of their conduct or even free to have legally recognized civil unions or to obtain employee benefits as dependents. Feminists will not give up until homosexuality is entitled to the full sanction of law. This is not about rights, but about dictating social mores and quashing dissent. With homosexual marriage, it cannot be gainsaid that the feminist movement has gone far beyond any interest in securing for women respect or equality. In plain bald point of fact, homosexuality has nothing to do with the rights or standing of women. The push to confer upon homosexual unions the status of marriage by feminists is instead intended as a leftist measure to further redefine marriage away from any of its traditional hallmarks as the fundamental building block of a cohesive society.

As alluded to previously, given that modern divorce laws and accepted modern cultural norms have virtually ensured that marriage, as an institution, has little of the strength and dignity that it once had (notwithstanding that many individual marriages may themselves be strong and dignified), it is now quite difficult to adequately defend the solemnity of marriage as a general matter. When people can be seen traipsing in and out of so-called "marriages" that endure for shorter periods than it takes for a movie to proceed from the theater to the DVD clearance bin, one can hardly lay claim to the principle that marriage is serious business, and that tampering with it is not a venture lightly undertaken. In short, marriage has been so doggedly defined down and undermined in the last 50 years that it is now but a short step to hammering that final nail in its coffin by adding homosexual unions to the mix. And, as noted previously, given modern feminism's express, pointed, vocal, and very savage assault on the institution of marriage itself, one must question why it is so utterly important for feminists to confer what they regard as the highly dubious benefits of marriage upon homosexual couples. Is it because feminists believe homosexuals are entitled to the same misery as heterosexual women? That hardly seems to be a victorious strike for equality.

In some ways, the homosexual community should justly feel insulted by the feminist "assistance" to their cause in this regard. It is precisely as though feminists took the institution of marriage, watered it down into an insipid broth, and then generously offered: "Here you go, and feast upon it!" Feminism has succeeded only so far in rendering the institution of marriage meaningless that they now welcome the homosexual community to further tamper with it. In all honesty, it is difficult to fathom why the homosexual community tolerates feminist patronage . . . er, matronage. . . in this matter, except, one may conjecture, for the fact that feminists represent, for them, a politically powerful sheltering port in a very dicey storm.

At the same time, there is logic to the feminist preoccupation with homosexual marriage. It is, in some ways, the perfect iconic symbol of the feminist movement. Within the homosexual relationship, there are no worries about one sex dominating another, no questions of "reproductive control": a truly equal and fruitless partnership. Heaven forbid that men and women should actually love one another and learn to get along with one another, to work through and respect their differences to make life work and to make each other happy. With homosexuality, people can just avoid all that trouble, all those differences, and all that grappling with stereotypes and traditional roles by hoisting those problems out the window. Homosexuality presents the perfect excuse for being completely intolerant of the opposite sex.

Opposing homosexual marriage, of course, is not the same thing as saying that society must outlaw homosexual conduct, or that homosexuals deserve legal discrimination. While many people unequivocally believe homosexuality is immoral, the fact remains that it is a highly dubious proposition that the law should govern human behavior in all respects. Moral convictions must frequently stand upon their own merit. But surely, homosexuals should be capable of comprehending the argument that it is unproductive and unhealthy to advance as a social "fact" the idea that sex is without biological meaning or purpose.

But perhaps even more important as a cultural issue, it should not be advanced as a social norm that, ahead of any other trait, an individual's sexual preferences are a sufficient or even desirable way to define and project one's self onto the public. Just as the implied suggestion of raunchy sex, flaunted openly by vulgar men and women, only serves to cheapen and demean sex and invite scorn, publicly flaunted homosexuality has no legitimate claim to respect. No matter how much the homosexual community may complain about it or scream "Bigot!," people can hardly be faulted for showing distaste or disgust toward those individuals within the homosexual community who (unfortunately for many homosexuals, surely) have sought to become the face of homosexuality in America, and who have chosen to define themselves solely by virtue of their sexual tastes. Men wearing jewelry and make-up and acting and talking and dressing in a conspicuously effeminate manner, or women cropping their hair, wearing unbecoming clothing, and acting masculine in deliberate and conspicuous rejection of their natural qualities, do not by any stretch command admiration of their own merit. It is ridiculous that anyone in the homosexual community should imagine that homosexuality, by itself, is a legitimate basis on which reverence should be due—*from anyone*.

The purposeful projection of homosexuality, that "in-your-face" militancy or conspicuous cross-behavior exhibited by one contingent of the homosexual community, by itself suggests that homosexuality for them is not a private matter at all, but a political matter. It is a statement of defiance and of rejection (and, incidentally, of insecurity), and in many ways it is an expression of hatred toward those who do not agree with or condone their behavior. They are openly daring and inviting confrontation and opposition, and it is the height of hypocrisy for them to be surprised or affronted when such opposition manifests itself. Such behavior legitimately commands (and almost begs for) the opposite of respect: pity.

One encounters any number of homosexuals—whether known or unknown—for whom their sexual inclinations are primarily a private matter. Many homosexual individuals quite properly define and project themselves by reference to other more significant personal attributes—traits such as intelligence, compassion, and humor, for example—that ensure that there is, in contrast to the militant contingent, a common ground upon which differences in moral outlook serve as no barrier whatsoever to productive, congenial, and affectionate relationships. Thus, disapproval of homosexuality does not mean that one must dislike homosexual individuals. But there is no reason anyone must respect or approve of homosexuality simply because it is homosexuality. Homosexuality is not an achievement.

This is precisely why homosexual marriage creates such a firestorm of debate. For those who have moral objections to homosexuality, the marriage issue requires not tolerance of private immorality, but approval of public immorality. And one's objections need not even be moral. Even more than casual sex, this institutionalizing of homosexual marriage is manifestly directed toward the further de-sexing of the sexes. Normalization of homosexuality unmistakably advances a cultural mindset that neuters women and castrates men; sex becomes meaningless in a biological sense. While this judgment sounds harsh and even extreme, it is the unvarnished reality.

This further effort to de-sex women advanced by feminism seems an awfully wrong-headed way of getting back at men or achieving sexual equality. But it is no wonder that feminists feel a kinship with the push to legitimize homosexuality. As discussed above, having eliminated the idea that men serve any useful or meaningful role in society and having removed from sex any purpose outside of selfish sexual gratification, the lesbian couple represents, to a certain degree, the feminist ideal. And because gay men have no interest in women biologically, they receive the feminists' wholehearted endorsement because gay men are the only men by which the feminists do not feel threatened in their rabid quest to "control their own reproduction."

Yet, given that there are so many things that can be championed on behalf of *all* women in our society, it seems more than a little disheartening that the modern feminist movement invests so much of its time and effort in this pursuit. In virtually every manifestation of their political aims, feminists seem intent upon working toward the irrelevancy of women as women. If the feminists succeed in convincing women, as a rule, to eschew any interest in shouldering the responsibilities of their sex, then women are bound to become much *less* important than they were in a society that supposedly oppressed them. This is not good for women either individually, or as a group. And this is nowhere exhibited more clearly than in today's *raison d'etre* of the feminist movement: abortion.

Chapter Twenty-One: Nurturing Young Women With the Message of Fear, Isolation, and Despair

When we consider that women are treated as property, it is degrading to women that we should treat our children as property to be disposed of as we see fit.

--Elizabeth Cady Stanton

To my certain knowledge this crime is not confined to those whose love of ease, amusement and fashionable life leads them to desire immunity from the cares of children: but is practiced by those whose inmost souls revolt from the dreadful deed, and in whose hearts the maternal feeling is pure and undying.

--Susan B. Anthony

It has been nearly 40 years since the Supreme Court's 1973 decision in *Roe v. Wade.* *Roe* created a Constitutional right to abortion—"created," because the no such right existed in American jurisprudence before the *Roe* decision. And while this long-standing precedent may withstand legal challenge at this late date, the abortion question very much remains, and for good reason. It is arguably the single most critical moral issue confronting America, or the world, today. Since morality, at its root, is about the rules that should be employed to govern human relationships, abortion could be said to encompass the whole of the moral universe: of what value is human life?

As stated previously in this book, abortion persists in being the flagship issue on which almost every other feminist issue rides. And while there are many people who would not describe themselves as feminists who nevertheless support abortion "rights," and even some feminists who oppose abortion, it is, in common understanding, the single issue on which a feminist defines herself as a feminist. The modern feminist falls on the abortion-rights side of the divide.

The facts on abortion are sobering: today, abortion is basically used as means of birth control, not significantly different from the use of condoms or other contraceptives. According to the Center for Bioethical Reform, the number of abortions can be conceptualized as a lifetime average of one abortion per woman worldwide. In the U.S. alone, over 1.2 million abortions are performed annually, meaning roughly *3300 abortions occur daily* in this country.

With those kinds of numbers, the issue is in desperate need of honest assessment, but not merely for moral reasons. It is in desperate need of evaluation because those numbers indicate that an incredibly large proportion of women are exercising questionable judgment, and engaging in seriously irresponsible behavior. The bottom line for women, and therefore feminism, should be: do we really want our daughters, sisters, wives or mothers to go through this experience? Is it right to isolate our daughters, sisters, wives, and mothers when faced with a decision whether or not to abort their own babies? And finally: Are you kidding?

Let's take a step back. It has to be acknowledged that the debate that one sees regularly in the news and political arenas is not a debate at all. A debate is a reasoned argument by two parties taking opposing positions on a single question. So there is no debate. Feminists repeatedly hammer on the matter of legal rights, and pro-life proponents generally talk about morality. But in point of fact, the one need not have anything to do with the other. After all, our society allows any number of immoral activities to occur without legal sanction; there is plenty of lying, stealing, cheating, fornicating, adultery, and what-not that the law steers well clear of. In fact, one could argue that both sides could have their way if they fully appreciated and accepted the fundamental differences between their respective positions: abortion is morally wrong, but we are willing to allow it to occur legally because it suits some other expedient social need.

But that resolution is completely dissatisfying to most Americans. We Americans like to think of ourselves not merely as free, but as *good*. Strangely enough, however, that describes precisely the current impasse: abortion is legal, but morally abhorrent. And while that statement may generate some resistance, there is no getting around the fact that the issue is a moral one. Feminists have worked hard to channel the abortion issue into arguments about the law and rights because it distracts people from the reality of what abortion is, and it helps them avoid confronting the deeper implications about the effects of abortion on society in general, and on women, in particular, of having made it commonplace. Even more, feminists understand that the only way to sell abortion as "good" is to cast it as though it embodies the virtue of liberty and self-determination. But at its heart, abortion is not about rights; it is about the fundamental values and priorities upheld by our culture, and about the virtues and vices we recognize in our human condition. Abortion is about the choices we make with regard to the value of other human beings, and what those choices reveal about our character, both individually and collectively as a society.

In that moral realm, feminism is without ammunition. Before the point that an egg and sperm unite, there is no such thing as life. But once the egg is fertilized, without drastic intervention (or natural disruption), the normal and natural result is the birth of a living human being. No matter how much one rationalizes the motivations for abortion, and no matter how much feminists attempt to infuse cold biological terms into the dialog, there is no getting around the fact that life begins at conception because it really cannot begin anywhere else. Abortion does not prevent or "undo" what has already happened. Without question, abortion terminates life.

Thus, the feminist position is not about where "life" begins, whatever they may claim, but about where "personhood" begins. In the feminist view, life that exists in the womb has no claim to personhood. This, by itself, should give anyone pause. After all, while the unborn life is surely greatly dependent (and, at the beginning, wholly dependent) upon the mother for its survival, and obviously lacks other characteristics of independent viability, the idea that that dependency or inferior functionality can negate personhood is a very dangerous argument. It is precisely why, for example, the abortion question leads to euthanasia and eugenics issues. If society is willing to decide that "life" is not the key issue, but rather "personhood," then it opens the door up to the idea that people can arbitrarily define what "personhood" requires. It allows people to place all individuals on a scale in which each has a differing claim of worthiness to life or, indeed, to other benefits. In fact, it is precisely the mindset that has allowed slavery and other inhumanities to persist—including treating women as inferior or expendable. If a living human can be defined as something less than a "person," and if those lesser humans are not entitled to the same legal protections or rights as other humans, then the result is inescapable that we must embrace a moral relativism that is dependent not upon some universal principle, but only upon majority sentiment. It justifies the sort of prejudices and persecutions that feminists have earnestly professed that they abhor.

Even more, the dependency issue illustrates why it is difficult for anyone to take seriously attempts to divert the discussion into questions of viability (that is, when a child may survive without biological dependence on the mother), insofar as viability is intended to somehow pacify moral misgivings about abortion. For example, Professor Peter Singer at Princeton has questioned why one may not therefore "abort" a child until it reaches the age of, say, one year, on the theory that young babies are no more capable of surviving on their own than are fetuses. His argument is a natural outcropping of the viability argument, and it is philosophically difficult to distinguish his position from the viability principle relied upon by abortion advocates.

Interestingly, though, while feminists strongly—and disingenuously—argue that "moral" questions are necessarily religious (which they are not) and therefore have no place in civic policy (which is a fallacy), they nevertheless refuse to admit that what they are advocating is concededly immoral even in the religious realm that they reject. Instead, they have attempted to convince everyone that abortion either has no moral aspect, or, more forcefully, that "individual conscience" is a sufficient substitute for universally acceptable moral standards. Just on the face of it, the "individual conscience" argument is a highly peculiar position to take for a group that is intent on reinventing social values, even if it is a very convenient cop-out for politicians who lack the spine to advocate, let alone harbor, any personal moral convictions. If "individual consciences" were sufficient to resolve questions of morality, it would seem that the feminists have no leg to stand on with respect to a single social position they have taken, whether that is sexism, abortion, homosexuality, or anything else.

The reason feminists rigidly insist that a woman's "individual conscience" is the only relevant consideration is based upon their need to keep up the pretense that their position is not *immoral*, but *amoral*. That is, by claiming that the feminist movement itself is morally neutral, it can place the entire moral burden upon the individual woman who is faced with an unplanned pregnancy. Even though feminists advocate that abortion should be permitted under almost any circumstance whatsoever—at any stage of pregnancy, decided unilaterally by any woman no matter her age, and for any reason solely at her own discretion—they nevertheless can absolve themselves from any moral culpability. Feminism isolates women who choose abortion, essentially telling them: "We did not tell you to do it or force you to do it, we just gave you the right to do it." Feminism can wash its hands of the dreadful emotional and spiritual fallout that many women face both before and after having an abortion.

As mentioned above, by isolating the moral aspect of abortion by claiming that it is a matter of individual conscience rather than public policy, feminists can claim that this personal moral vice is in their alternate reality a public civic virtue of "liberty." But even on its face, abortion is clearly not about one person's "rights." Abortion necessarily involves at least three individuals: the child, the mother, and the father.

Of course, when it comes to abortion, feminists have almost completely succeeded in dispensing with fathers. And while pro-life factions have attempted to address the interests of a father in his own offspring, that consideration has not materialized into anything legally concrete except for a handful of spousal notification statutes in some states. And while such statutes can put minor roadblocks in the way of women who want an abortion, abortion activists have succeeded almost completely in removing the interests of fathers from any legal status with respect to their unborn children, even when the father is married to the mother. It is only when a child is born that feminists want to assert that the father may yet have some legal rights—or, more to the point, legal obligations. (Incidentally, it should be noted that, after doing their utmost to marginalize men with respect to pregnancy, feminists have been met with the natural and normal result of their misguided policies: there is virtually a nationwide epidemic of divorced and single fathers shirking their child-support and child-raising responsibilities.) Under the feminists' perverse rationale, fathers have been removed almost entirely from the abortion question.

The other participant in this issue that gets short shrift by feminists is the child. And while the pro-life side clearly has the moral high ground on this point, it too often focuses upon the simple argument that human life, once brought into existence, is entitled to legal protection. But it can rationally be argued, even if not always entirely morally justified, that there can be exceptions to that argument. Thus, the more accurate statement of the pro-life position is that human life should never be taken without some morally valid reason. And in the overwhelming majority of abortion cases, the reasons invoked by women are not morally compelling in the least.

Consequently, the real moral focus must be on the culpability of the mother. And once the focus is placed upon the mother, the bleakness of the feminist position becomes apparent in so many contexts. Feminists do not merely expect society to exalt the mother's reasons, whatever they may be, over any other consideration, they outright demand it. In the feminist perspective, a woman's subjective determination about the value of the life her own child, however ill-founded, flimsy, or incorrect, is deemed to be paramount to any conceivable interest that society could assert. This, to a certain extent, is the defining characteristic of the feminist ideal: freeing women entirely from any social or moral responsibility to society and to the human race. Thus, in this one issue, it is apparent that what is at stake for feminists is not truly "choice," but the moral and social corruption of young women. Frequently, the reasons invoked by women to obtain abortions are almost universally reasons that, in a humanitarian sense, should militate *against* abortion. That is, in a humanitarian world, one does not simply kill people because there is not enough food, love, or care for them. Instead, compassion should compel us to find the food, love, and care that people need.

Because the real question is one of *justifiable* rationales, it is very easy to deflect false arguments cast by feminists, such as when they raise the issues of medical necessity or rape. In cases of medical necessity, where one or both lives are at serious risk if the pregnancy continues, it is morally acceptable to place the decision in the hands of the mother as the only person capable of exercising her will, and no moral blame attaches where one innocent life *must* be sacrificed in order for another innocent life to survive. This principle generally holds true with respect to any two people in a comparable survival situation. In addition, one might rationally argue that women who obtain an abortion when they have become pregnant as a result of rape have an understandable and defensible inability to cope with the burdens and stigma of an unwanted pregnancy. In either case, while the lives of the children in question are innocent, the mother's considerations are entitled to some special regard. However, even so, there are valid arguments to be made that abortion is not necessarily a sound option for the victims of rape, notwithstanding feminist's reliance upon rape as a universally legitimate justification for abortion. Post-abortion counselors have commented on the fact that women who have abortions subsequent to rape often feel tremendous guilt for having compounded the trauma of the original crime by turning around and victimizing an innocent being themselves.

But truly, feminist arguments based on rape, incest, and so on, are simply window-dressing. For the most part, abortion activists are not really interested in the whys and wherefores at all. They focus the issue solely on "rights," and respond to every attempt to restrict abortion by being offended at the notion that anyone would try to "take away" a woman's "rights." This is an effective strategy, because it serves to divert attention from the fact that almost no rationale invoked by women to justify abortion is sound, let alone compelling. And although pro-choice proponents like to focus on how important it is for abortion to be legal by citing to cases of medical necessity, rape, or abuse what about the other roughly 95-plus percent of abortions?

To put it in practical terms, there are several contexts under which a woman might consider abortion: she is single, and does not want to raise a child; she is married, but for reasons of her own she does not want a child or another child; she is married, but for reasons of their own, a couple decides they do not want a child or another child; she is married or single, and decides that the child is of an unwanted sex, or suffers from some physical defect. From a pro-life standpoint, naturally, none of these rationales justify the killing of an unborn child. And truthfully, none do. That is because, while the above contexts supply the *circumstances* under which an abortion might be sought, none supply an actual *justification*.

Women faced with an unwanted pregnancy are under no compulsion to raise their unborn children, particularly when there are so many couples who pray for the opportunity to adopt a newborn baby. Consequently, the conclusion is inescapable that abortion is chosen by pregnant women not because their *child* is unwanted, but because the *pregnancy itself* is unwanted. Why? The only rational answer is because pregnancy carries with it a very obvious physical manifestation. Women who are pregnant but do not want their child *also do not want anyone to know that they are pregnant*. Consequently, feminists, in advocating a "right" to abortion, are really offering something else: they are offering to women the ability to be freed from having to face the public consequences of their private conduct. They are offering deception and secrecy.

Notwithstanding the "triumphs" of the sexual revolution, sexual activity that results in an unwanted pregnancy still carries with it a social and moral stigma. As discussed previously, this is a result of the contradictory standards under which we live: while everyone seems quite willing to accept that sexual activity is occurring with indiscriminate frequency, they nevertheless are unwilling to face up to the fact that such activity has a perfectly normal result—pregnancy. And many pregnancies are unwanted for the very simple reason that many women are engaging in sexual activity without intending (or probably even imagining, in some cases) that they would get pregnant, and without the slightest interest in bearing the child of the men with whom they choose to have sex. Consequently, many women terminate their pregnancies because they do not want to confront someone else's judgment—their partner's, their family's, or their social circle's—upon their own moral folly in engaging in sex outside of marriage, for engaging in sex with someone to whom they have no serious or longstanding emotional attachment, for their lack of prudence in failing to utilize birth control measures with appropriate diligence, for their character in willingly giving away their own child, or any combination of these motives. And while these rationales for hiding pregnancy may be perfectly understandable, they are not morally compelling.

Although it has become occasionally stylish for successful single women to decide to have a child on their own as a "lifestyle choice"—such as the infamous "Murphy Brown" character from television—such women often do so in very public ways, so that their pregnancies are free (so they imagine) from accusations of carelessness or depravity. Thus, Madonna made her first proud single-motherhood pregnancy very public, and actresses whose biological clocks are getting long in the tooth frequently make no bones about their pregnancy quests. But rarely do we see girls or women (let alone their boyfriends) proudly owning up to a common, plain old exercise of inferior judgment and lack of control accompanied by a willingness to shoulder the consequences of their conduct.

Consequently, the real hypocrisy of the pro-abortion stance is that it directly and forcefully reinforces and validates the very same puritan ethos that condemns abortion as immoral: abortion implicitly, but unmistakably, acknowledges the *shame* of the predicament. In the feminist "looking glass" world, indiscriminate sex is nothing to be ashamed of, but bearing a child from an unintended and unwanted pregnancy is—as though the two have nothing whatsoever to do with one another. Abortion is thus intended to abet women who seek to conceal their shame. This is a remarkably strange position for a movement that purports to reject Judeo-Christian morality as irrelevant or narrow-minded.

As stated above, abortion rationales related to not wanting a child are without serious merit; bearing a child does not require rearing it. Abortion is not about rejecting motherhood, it is about rejecting pregnancy: about women hiding from the world their own conduct and the fact that they don't want their own child. And the reason this secrecy is so necessary is that society and tradition still venerate motherhood, for perfectly good and sound reasons. A woman who does not want her own child and who therefore willfully terminates the life of her own flesh and blood presents a glimpse of humanity that is seriously morally and socially troubling. It is hard to imagine something more *unnatural* than a mother who rejects her own offspring; it is life-negating, and is diametrically opposed to the instinctive quest for survival.

This is precisely why, despite the frequency with which abortions occur in this country, and notwithstanding thirty-plus years of "choice" rhetoric, abortion usually remains a shameful and sordid secret that women might share only with a few close and sympathetic friends or family members, or never share at all. Having to admit to an abortion usually means having to confront the very same judgment the abortion was aimed at avoiding. And although older women may now and then publicly admit to having had an abortion in their youth, it is still nothing to be proud of. As a matter of fact, some women, such as those who belong to the "Silent No More" Awareness Campaign, admit to it precisely because they feel a need to expose their shame and regret in an effort to warn other young women of the folly of treating abortion as though it presents an easy "solution" to an unwanted pregnancy. Consequently, it ends up being feminists themselves who insist that abortion remain a matter of secrecy and isolation; it is pro-choice feminists who are doing the most to preserve the stigma of both an unwanted pregnancy and an abortion. By offering abortion as the solution to a dilemma, the feminist movement hypocritically signals its implicit agreement with society's established standard that having an *unwanted* pregnancy is something women, in most cases, ought to be ashamed of.

Even more, the pro-choice mantra that all children should be "wanted" reveals something about what is not said: all "unwanted" children should be aborted. And how do they define these terms? "Wanted," to them, is not entirely based upon the subjective viewpoint of the mother, but is instead defined according to a certain idealized social structure. Thus, while they purport to promote "choice," at the same time, they subtly reinforce those social pressures that would guide that choice toward abortion. Thus, for example, a pregnant unmarried teenager is regarded as "socially irresponsible" if she does not opt for abortion. Abortion proponents are frequently, if not always, in agreement with population growth advocates who encourage the idea that families, and particularly poor families, should not have a lot of children, and they promote abortion as a means of birth control in third world countries under the banner of protecting children from poverty and starvation. Rather than seeing these problems as part of our moral or humanitarian responsibilities to address, they naively contend that these social problems could be avoided if certain people would just stop having children.

Margaret Sanger's original intent in starting Planned Parenthood (originally, the American Birth Control League) was to advance her pet philosophy of eugenics. It is still being advanced. In fact, for pro-choice organizations, the ready availability of taxpayer-funded abortion services for the poor is claimed as part and parcel of the "right," a proposition that is unique in American political philosophy. As elaborated upon above, to feminist proponents of abortion, a "right" means more than simply a freedom; to them, it creates an entitlement. Thus, what they are really advocating is the idea that certain people *should be* aborting their offspring.

If abortion were truly about independent choice, feminists would be silent on the social implications of childbirth and population, but they are not. Abortion is a means of keeping society "orderly," and encourages the elitist notion that only certain people, such as those who have the wherewithal to raise children "properly" or who otherwise exhibit social stability, ought to procreate. Thus, again, the irony: feminists generally believe it is better that responsible couples have children, which is, to some degree, the same position as moral fundamentalists. But they disagree drastically upon the means.

So where does that leave women faced with unwanted pregnancies? Unfortunately, in a very unpalatable predicament. No one wants to publicly acknowledge a private folly. And, as stated previously, American society, for all that sex is everywhere, is still remarkably prudish. Because pregnancy manifests itself within months, young women have a short time frame in which to make a "choice." That time pressure adds to the other fears and social pressures that weigh upon their decision-making. The "choice" argument is effective precisely because it can exploit these vulnerabilities. Further, at the same time that feminists seek to reinforce the social pressures that make abortion appealing, they have worked assiduously to isolate women from any influences which might militate against abortion. For example, feminists always come out in strong opposition to parental notification laws.

Let's be clear: parental notification laws apply only in the case of minors—that is, girls who are under 18 years of age. According to the Guttmacher Institute, roughly 17 percent of all abortions are obtained by girls in their teens. Since 18 and 19 year olds account for two-thirds of all teen pregnancies, parental notification would apply only in a small subset of abortions. Claims made by feminists that parental notification laws are designed to abolish altogether the "reproductive rights" of women are greatly overstated. Notwithstanding that, the battle on this front is very telling.

To start, on their face, parental notification laws serve two purposes. First, parents have a perfectly valid and tremendously strong interest in their children's health. Given that a doctor may not even administer a vaccination without a signed consent (after full disclosure) from a parent, and that schools may not distribute a single aspirin or a cough drop without a parent's consent, it is frankly appalling that parents may be kept unaware of a major surgical procedure being performed upon their minor child. It is hard to imagine that any parent, pro-choice or pro-life, would be happy to discover that their minor daughter underwent an abortion without their knowledge, let alone consent. Second, notification allows parents the opportunity to influence the decision of their minor child.

Feminists inevitably claim that the danger of parental notification is the threat that a parent will react with physical violence to news of his or her minor daughter's pregnancy and/or choice to abort. And while this may be a legitimate concern, no one has actually tried to quantify how real that threat is—that is, how likely it is that the notification would result in actual physical injury. It surely has happened, but it may be that it is as common as the number of times a minor has suffered medical complications from an abortion, requiring additional medical care (where, ironically, the parent's consent is required). In other words, the risk of injury from retaliation may not be any higher than the risk of injury from abortion. But more to the point, any concerns over physical retaliation can easily be addressed; for example, a law could be drafted so that a minor who is concerned for her safety is entitled to have a law enforcement officer or Child Protective Services representative accompany her to deliver a parental notification. In the end, the retaliation argument seems to be an exceedingly thin basis on which to override the critical interests of parents in overseeing medical treatment of their minor children.

And strangely, of course, the "pro-choice" feminists do not seem to be particularly concerned about the consequences of parental notification when a minor's "choice" is to keep her child—where, as a practical matter, notification generally occurs in 100 percent of the cases. Why should parental notification become an unbearable burden for "choice" proponents only when that choice is abortion? The answer is because the threat of physical retaliation is just a diversion from the real problem feminists have with parental notification.

The fact is, a significant number of Americans have an ethical problem with abortion. Even those who consider themselves pro-choice have a qualm or two about unrestricted abortion-on-demand, and might find themselves conflicted if confronted by their own pregnant minor daughter. It is often much easier to support an idea in the abstract than the concrete. And that is really the point. Parental notification does not suit the "choice" crowd because it lets the cat out of the bag. Parental notification laws expose the secret that is often the whole point of obtaining an abortion in the first place. Furthermore, notification negates the wedge of distrust, shame, and secrecy that adolescent sexual activity, pregnancy, and abortion creates between young girls and their parents—a wedge pro-choice proponents have no scruple about encouraging. The pro-choice argument, on its face, should strike anyone as exceedingly troublesome in what it says about the feminist perspective on parents. Unequivocally, pro-choice feminists take the position that parents should be regarded generally not as the protectors of their children, but as inherently untrustworthy and abusive in regard to their own children.

It is sad to say, but, again according to the Guttmacher institute, 70 percent of American women who obtain abortions identify themselves as Christian (either Protestant or Catholic). While the statistics do not reveal how many minors obtaining abortion are Christian, if one simply assumes that the same ratio applies, then 70 percent of the minors who obtain abortions have been raised in Christian families—that is, in a general sense, families in which it is considered immoral not only to abort a child, but to engage in sexual intercourse outside of marriage.

It is not difficult to imagine that these girls would be quite reluctant to reveal their pregnancies to their parents. Because abortion provides a means by which these young women do not have to reveal their sexual activity, parental notification completely undermines "choice." With notification, the primary driving motivation for obtaining an abortion simply disappears. Even more, one would reasonably expect that, in Christian families, the parents would be strongly opposed to abortion, and would try to exercise their influence to dissuade their daughters from getting one, notwithstanding the shame that might accompany pregnancy. Consequently, feminists oppose parental notification laws not because they impact rights, necessarily, or because they would result in injury, but because they may impact, overall, the ultimate choice that may be made. Accordingly, the pro-choice lobby has a vested interest in insuring that abortion be characterized as a personal and private choice, made by the woman in complete moral, spiritual, and often literal, isolation.

There is another significant implication of the fact that so many women who obtain abortions identify themselves as Christian. While feminists occasionally point out this statistic as though it reveals some great hypocrisy, the truth is much grimmer, and more troubling. It is not that all these women *pretend* to consider abortion immoral, it is that many *do* believe abortion is immoral but, for one reason or another, obtain one anyway. Thus, for them, abortion is a significant moral transgression, and the results can be psychologically and spiritually devastating. The fact of an abortion becomes a burdensome, daunting, and dirty little secret that they may never have the courage to reveal to anyone.

Of course, even women who are not Christian, who truly believe that abortion has no moral character, can easily find themselves troubled by an abortion. This is particularly true when they eventually have children, or decide to have children but encounter difficulties with pregnancies or births, when their babies experience health problems, or if they find out that they cannot have children. Suddenly, an aborted child can take on an overwhelming significance, even years or decades later, both physically and psychologically. These effects are well-documented by organizations that engage in post-abortion counseling, and they are yet another facet of the problem with abortion that is utterly ignored and glossed over by abortion's feminist supporters. In fact, the entire pro-choice contingent, for the most part, denies that any such effects exist.

For example, NOW has asserted that "post-abortion depression . . . [is] a fallacious condition" and elsewhere denies that "women experience psychological trauma after terminating a pregnancy." Nowhere in the feminist agenda is there attention paid to either physical or mental after-effects of abortion, and NOW disingenuously defends its denial by claiming that "no credible studies" exist on the existence of a psychological condition called "post-abortion syndrome," although the organization is also on record as opposing that the National Institute of Health carry out such a study. NOW seems to hang its hat on the assertion that, simply because the after-effects of abortion have not been given the status of an "official" psychological condition, no women experience any trauma related to abortion at all. They maintain this fiction even though scores of post-abortion counseling organizations exist across the nation, and these organizations do not seem to have any shortage of women lining up to obtain their services.

Alternatively, feminists argue that the psychological problems encountered by women after an abortion are no different from what they might experience after having an unwanted child—as though pregnancy is simply a disease women suffer and over which they have no control. Again, it is not feminists, but usually community and faith-based groups that try to help troubled women, while feminists steadfastly deny that women need help. One notable exception to this rule is a group called Exhale, a pro-choice organization that engages in post-abortion counseling. Exhale alone has served over 15,000 women on its hotline, and admits that it has tremendous difficulty obtaining funding—because the sources that fund pro-choice organizations, for the most part, *refuse to admit that abortion has any negative psychological outfall.*

While not every woman who experiences an abortion may suffer regret or guilt, those who do find that feminists are unsympathetic, even when a woman is pro-choice. Feminists are so narrowly focused upon their desperate grip to keep abortion legal that they cannot afford to admit that serious physiological and psychological problems can accompany the procedure or to admit that there are problems related to abortion that are in serious need of being addressed. For example, while NOW triumphantly boasted that several parental notification statutes had been defeated in the 2008 elections, it never acknowledged, let alone offered any solutions for, the problems and anguish of parents who may be left to deal with a daughter's post-abortion medical complications, or their suicidal, abused, traumatized, or statutorily raped daughters. And despite the feminists' otherwise wholesale condemnation of men, one is hard-pressed to find anything negative said about men who pressure or force their reluctant and emotionally vulnerable girlfriends to obtain abortions because they haven't got the fortitude to face up to their responsibilities as men.

Adverse information relating to why women obtain abortions and what happens to women who have undergone an abortion is dismissed by pro-choice feminists as false, overblown, or negligible, and post-abortion problems are chalked up to other causes such as failed relationships, a poor family life, or the unplanned pregnancy—but never the abortion itself. Even if one were to take the pro-choice feminists at their word and allow that depression after an abortion is merely symptomatic of other psychological difficulties, it strains credibility to claim that abortion has no effect, or, as some feminists claim, has only beneficial effects such as the feeling of relief. If nothing else, one would think feminism would be concerned that so many women have such serious and unresolved mental health issues which, strangely enough, only seem to manifest their intensity after an abortion. Only in the feminist world is abortion no more consequential to young women than a procedure to treat a hangnail, but at the same time so emotionally and morally grave and burdensome to young women that they cannot, under any circumstances, be forced to tell their parents about it.

The issue has been so politicized that the public conflict presents two mutually exclusive truths: abortion is meaningless, or it is soul-destroying. And because of its political character, most serious, sober, honest, and open analysis of the problems that lead some women to seek out an abortion or the problems that abortions can create or exacerbate is quashed by abortion's proponents. In this information vacuum, abortion has become a fact of modern life in America for young women. The statistics are appalling: 8 out of every 1000 women in this country (of all ages) are getting an abortion *every year*; and 2 out of every 100 girls in America between the ages of 15 and 19 are getting an abortion *every year*. While these numbers seem insignificant, it must be borne in mind that a woman's fertility generally spans three to four decades, and that roughly half the women in this country at any time are not of child-bearing (either pre- or post-) age. Thus, in real numbers, it may be that the average comes closer to one out of every three or four women in the country obtains an abortion in her lifetime, or even higher. This not only signifies a tremendous amount of sexual activity in women (and men) who are unwilling and unprepared to accept the responsibility of parenthood, it also does not bode well for the mental and physical health and well-being of thousands of women—and, consequently, for the well-being of society as a whole. Is this really what a "woman's movement" should be promoting? It is hard to justify a feminism that both staunchly refuses to gather facts and sweeps adverse but critically relevant information about this issue under the carpet because it undermines its broader agenda—no matter the cost to real women.

But feminists are politically realistic. It is only by flatly denying, despite evidence to the contrary, that abortion is consequential to women that they have been able to prevail to the degree that they have. As discussed previously, the feminist movement has been hugely successful in promoting abortion by forcing the discourse away from the substance of the real problems of what abortion is, why women undergo an abortion, and how abortion affects women, into a discussion only of rights and legalities. And when it comes to that, the game may be over. Forty years after *Roe v. Wade*, regardless of how poor or wrong that decision was as a constitutional matter, the principle of *stare decisis*—a legal doctrine under which the Supreme Court will let even poorly reasoned precedents stand if they would result in serious social or political upheaval—militates strongly in favor of letting it stand, even (and, to some extent, more so) with a constitutionally conservative court. With over 1.2 million abortions occurring yearly in this country, a legal shift now would have tremendous political and practical consequences.

Abortions happen very frequently, and many women who get them end up being uncomfortable with their decisions, even when they are they have no qualms about the legality of abortion. And this happens primarily because young women make this decision under conditions that generally do not lead to intelligent or rational decision-making: isolated, pressured by time, frightened, and devoid of information. This is true even when women are fully aware of and comfortable with the reasons they are seeking an abortion. The problem is that women find themselves in a situation in which it is very difficult to fully or rationally digest the ramifications of their decision, and the pro-choice movement has done little to address that issue. That is because the pro-choice movement is not selling abortion at all, it is selling a solution to a problem. The message of abortion proponents is: "We can make your problem magically disappear as though it never happened, with little pain or trouble and no one the wiser."

The reality, of course, is starkly different. Abortion is a cold, lonely, unpleasant, and sordid experience, and, rather than erasing a past mistake, it often adds another more grave one to the balance sheet, one that has to be carried in secret for years, if not for a lifetime. Plus, there is the added bonus of possible medical complications and psychological problems. If feminists were truly interested in the welfare of women, one would think they would work to make sure women's choices were fully informed by quantifying, studying, and disseminating information on these issues, and they would be particularly concerned about forcing such weighty decisions upon isolated minor girls who are motivated by fear, who have little practical knowledge of what is involved, and whose judgment is highly questionable. But pro-choice feminists have *no* interest in these matters, because *any* information on these points undermines the marketing message. Ignorance and secrecy are tools which ensure the perpetuation of abortion.

In the end, abortion as a "solution" for women is largely a fiction. Women are not "empowered" when they are deprived of the ability to make rational, informed decisions, and feminists' refusal to seriously acknowledge that any problems attend abortion suggests that feminist believe women cannot be trusted to make "good" decisions when given complete information. Even more critically, any culture that willingly and openly subscribes to the idea that engaging in sex is a meaningless recreational pastime cannot simultaneously adopt the position that pregnancy is extraordinary. Unless people confront the realities of our post-sexual revolution culture by either instituting a new (that is, old) cultural norm of sexual restraint, or, alternatively, removing, lessening, or negating the fear and social pressures that lead women to seek an abortion, women will continue on this cycle of self-defeat. The attempt to gloss over the very real dilemmas and personal crises created by abortion in the real world of women is unconscionable if what we are truly interested in is the well-being of women.

But what is truly astounding is how long feminists have been able to successfully peddle the abortion issue as one of sympathy and solidarity for the plight of young women. That posture would be more believable if they showed the slightest indication that they regarded the issue with the gravity it deserves, and addressed its sordid realities rather than passing it off under the smokescreens of discussing only "rights" and "reproductive control." With virtually every other issue, feminists (here, primarily radical feminists) do not hesitate to force-feed the public with aggressively graphic and tasteless emphasis on bodily parts and functions, such as when discussing or displaying the dubious artistic merits of "The Vagina Monologues" or lesbian sexual practices, but fall far short of admitting the graphic truth of abortion's bloody and dreadful reality.

It is not simply the fact of 1.2 million babies being aborted every year that is tragic, although that is certainly heartbreaking and damning enough on its own. It is also 1.2 million women, many of them scared, lonely, frightened, truly victimized, and misled, that cry out for our sympathy and our concern. Their welfare is not merely a matter of a temporary and immediate "problem" or "mistake" in need of a quick remedy. Their predicament is much more serious. They have been purposefully misled about the gravity and responsibility of governing their own lives. They are women who have already demonstrated poor judgment with respect to their sexual conduct, and they have very little concept of the ramifications, both physical and mental, to which they are subjecting themselves, first, in engaging in casual sex, and second, in making a decision to abort. Their decisions are reached not through rational and calm assessment with comprehensive information, supportive input, and loving counsel, but made in an environment of ignorance, emotional upheaval, and bewilderment. One need only seriously contemplate the baffling pro-choice bumper sticker: "If you cannot trust me with a choice, how can you trust me with a child?" It begs the very question it asks: it is precisely *because* women contemplating abortion have already demonstrated poor judgment with respect to making decisions about their own lives that they should not be trusted to have the power of life and death over another human being. Once an abortion takes place, there is no turning back—as many young women have come to realize in the cold and reflective light of day.

So long as feminists continue to succeed in framing the debate and veering it away from physical and social realities, abortion will continue to be employed, and it will continue to leave a path of troubled lives in its wake. But moral grandstanding, however justifiable, is not persuasive in a world in which morality has been overtaken by convenience. No woman in her right mind *desires* to go through the horrendous procedure of an abortion; no woman faces the prospect with cheer. The indifferent and even defiant face that feminism puts on the face of the abortion issue is a counterfeit courage; every sensible woman knows that face is a mask.

Abortion is not a small or meaningless act, and, contrary to what feminists claim, neither is it entirely private or personal. It has tremendous social implications. Not only does society have a valid interest in the welfare of children, it has a valid interest in the well-being of women, and it most assuredly has an interest in ensuring that our culture values life in all its manifestations. In the end, abortion reveals a great deal about the feminist mindset.

When it comes to women who obtain abortions because they freely engaged in sexual activity yet never spared sufficient thought to the possibility of getting pregnant, advocating abortion tells women that they need not face up to the normal and natural consequences of their actions. For women who are unwilling to accept the burden of raising a child, advocating abortion reinforces the feminist's pessimistic and anti-child message that having a child is the end of a young woman's hopes, dreams, and aspirations, and that selfishly taking the child's life and hiding one's weaknesses is better than enduring a well-earned humility to generously give that child up to adoption and a chance at a good life. For the youngest girls who undergo abortion under the unrelenting pressure of parents, boyfriends, or abusers, abortion reinforces the torment in which these girls are forced to suffer in secrecy and isolation. Rather than counseling confused young women to face their predicaments from the standpoint that life requires fortitude and maturity, that it demands that women face up to and shoulder errors and responsibilities, and that women should choose not to be governed by fear but by conviction and self-reliance, the feminist advocating abortion encourages young women to instead adopt hopeless, defeated, and shameful outlooks on themselves and on the world. By encouraging young women to resort to abortion to cover up their private conduct, rather than concede to the realities of their behavior and encourage society to take honest stock of what our cultural values are doing to young women, promoting abortion undermines the development of character traits that lead to strong and independent women. And even more critical to society overall, abortion means that women are as free to regard children as a burden or a mistake as much as an incarnation of love and hope. That perception has already seeped far too deeply into our cultural outlook.

There is no escaping this one truth: abortion is the supreme expression of despair. It is hard to imagine anything more hopeless, more soulless, more morbid, more sexless, than a mother who aborts the life of her own child for no better reason than that her child would interfere with her plans. This is the vision of womanhood feminism has given us.

CONCLUSION

What Has Feminism Really Done for Women Lately?

I'm just a person trapped inside a woman's body.

--Robin Morgan

Today, the modern feminist movement advocates nothing less than an overhaul of our culture, and tells the world that its goal is to make life better for women: to reshape our cultural values in ways that bestow upon women greater independence, greater respect, greater opportunity, and brighter futures. These are noble goals, and worthy goals. But the reality is that, while modern feminism has indeed overhauled our culture, it has not done so in ways that are designed to achieve these goals.

To modern feminism, the route to the betterment of women seems to follow a fairly inflexible formula. Women are encouraged to focus the majority of their energy upon dedication to a career, and particularly to achieve a leadership or ownership role in politics, business, or media; to avoid marriage or, if they should marry, to marginalize or ignore their husband's interests so that they do not interfere with their own; and to avoid the chaotic reality of children unless and until they have the independent wherewithal to place the primary responsibility for their children's care onto someone whose chief interest in the children's well-being may be a paycheck. Yet even a dyed-in-the-wool feminist might find it hard to achieve success and happiness with this formula when feminism constantly bombards women with the message that the world is inherently unfair and intent upon quashing every woman's ambitions. But more pertinently, this recipe is not one which vast numbers of women have any particular interest in following.

So where does that leave women? Unfortunately, modern feminism is not providing much in the way of workable, beneficial, constructive, and desirable solutions to many of the issues confronting women today. Make no mistake: there is a role for feminism to play in today's world. But it has to be a woman-focused feminism, one that appreciates and understands that women must play roles in society that are distinct from and yet harmonious with the roles that men play, and those roles must undertake critical responsibilities that are necessary for a healthy society.

When one takes a close look at many of the core ideas that the modern feminist movement is promoting, one cannot help but conclude that it is about trivializing, encouraging, and even institutionalizing a woman's basest inclinations and greatest failures, about surrendering the admittedly difficult burden of shouldering social responsibilities in return for the momentary ease and pleasure of a cowardly, weak, and indulgent self-centeredness. If a woman is frustrated in her marriage, feminism does not encourage or empower her to work toward improving and strengthening it for the betterment of herself, her family, and her community, it promotes giving in to divorce and condemning marriage and men. If young women are engaging in sex and getting pregnant or contracting diseases, feminism does not pull them up by the bootstraps and tell them to stop treating their bodies with so little respect. Instead it simply hands out contraception and abortion and sends women on their way, blissfully unconcerned with the fact that young women will continue to engage in self-destructive and self-defeating behavior. If a woman is facing hardship, feminism tells her it is not their problem, but that it is the government's duty to address her hardships and failings, and that she has no responsibility and no power to control her own fate. If a mother has trouble coping with the dilemma created by the emotional pull of wanting to raise her children versus the economic pull of trying to provide for those same children, feminism treats raising children as just another mundane household task, encouraging only the option that women should institutionalize their youngsters into facilities with state-dictated care standards. Feminism suggests that raising children is too limiting for intelligent women, expressly demeaning the role by suggesting that it can only be truly valued when it comes with a paycheck attached.

This mindset and these methods do not provide women a route to strength, independence, and influence. This is not what a group that advocates for women ought to be promoting. Where is the future, the hope, the promise of opportunity and liberation? Why is feminism so self-centered and self-limiting? Mostly: why is it so utterly negative in its outlook? Part of the reason is that feminism has been co-opted by leftist politics. It stopped being concerned about what women want and merit, and refocused the movement instead upon a false egalitarianism. It has adopted the idea that women can achieve something called "equality" by conquering their sexuality through the rejection of all the roles that naturally fall to women—in particular, by treating their sexuality as a cumbersome inconvenience, especially as it relates to the procreation and raising of their own children. It believes that if women can succeed in making themselves sexless, all people will behave and be treated as though they are the same: women will finally be equal to men. The modern feminist movement today is an unmitigated effort to cleanse women of being women.

This, in itself, is strange. One would think anything calling itself "feminism" would find strength in what womanhood is and to elevate it, rather than reject and demean it. But modern feminism's entire thrust is the rejection of what women have been and what they are. In a terrible irony, it has completely bought into the notion that women, as women, are essentially worthless. It encourages women to emulate and mimic the worst examples of chauvinistic masculinity in ways that men in western culture, for the most part, progressed away from centuries ago. Thus, modern feminism encourages women to belittle mothers as nothing more than "breeders" and "baby factories"; it denies and dismisses the problems of immature, sexually active, troubled young women by callously shunting them off to abortion clinics or the welfare rosters, treating them as expendable casualties of a corrupt ethic; it encourages women to be self-serving, to put their own well-being and ambitions above their spouse's and children's. If women, as a group, suffer when men treat them this way, how much worse is it when other women do the same to their own? The fact is, modern feminism only serves the interests of modern feminism; it does not serve the interests of women.

If women are to become truly strong and influential, to be a force for social good, at some point, they need to reject modern feminisms prejudices and its warped ideology and adopt the only position that will earn for women the independence, respect, and freedom that women allege that they want and deserve. It is the same position that any individual must take to achieve that same result: women have to be accountable, and to be held accountable. This means that women cannot blame the plight of women on someone else, and it means that they must willingly shoulder the responsibilities that society needs them to shoulder.

In order to have value, the end of any political endeavor ought to be to create opportunities for individuals to pursue their own fulfillment and to promote the overall betterment of ourselves and our society. But the feminist movement is not particularly interested in helping women to fulfill their own goals. Its pursuits are not primarily defined by reference to the best traits that women should exemplify and the highest ideals women should emulate. Instead, feminism is interested in defining and advancing an idealized political and legal paradigm of a woman, divorced entirely from what women actually are as physical, rational, emotional, and moral beings.

The manifest unhappiness, bitterness, and unrest of so many feminists should clue young women into the sheer despondency and liberal errors of following in their footsteps. Modern feminism's focus is not so much on what it hopes to achieve, but on what it aims to destroy. And while a life of rigid adherence to feminist prescriptions may suit some women, one too often seems to encounter the militant, defiant, and self-satisfied angst-ridden feminist, rather than the soul-felt joy of a woman who is at peace with who she is, what she has accomplished, and what she hopes to achieve in her life. Certainly, not every woman will find the same happiness by doing the same thing; after all, one of the beauties of our humanity is our very diverse interests and characters. But feminists are not interested in the diversity of women in the least, particularly since they are committed to the idea that women must deny the endowments with which nature has graced them. Overall, modern feminists refuse to accept the responsibilities of being women.

As long as men exist, as long as women exist, and as long as children are the promise of our future, it is utterly ridiculous for feminists to deny reality. Women need to recognize and embrace what it means to be female. This means to understand that women are different from men, and to appreciate that the difference is so fundamental that there is no meaning to the idea that men and women are "equal," except in specific legal or political contexts relating to how men and women should be treated. Socially, men and women will never be "equal" in the sense that they will ever be the same—nor should they be. Among other things, women need to stop trying to be anything other than women, to be happy about being women, and to be proud of being women. And most important among these is that feminism needs to respect motherhood and everything that the responsibility of motherhood entails.

There is no question that a movement focused upon the interests of women was necessary to bring about tremendous benefits for women in particular and for society in general. The opportunities available to women today to find and pursue their interests are unprecedented. But what started out as a movement that was interested in real problems and real solutions for women is now bogged down in an irrational and self-defeating ideology. There is still a need for a women's movement, but it must be focused upon women rather than upon political ideas of "equality," and it should seek to encompass all the roles that women can and should play in a productive and good society. It cannot continue to shoehorn women into modern feminism's crabbed and rigid projections of what women ought to be, a vision that is as oppressive to women as any witnessed throughout history.

History provides a long lens through which to evaluate our human character. And while many ideas have come and gone, the strength—and therefore, truth—of any idea must be measured by its power to persist in the face of change. Human character is surely flawed, and it is the height of arrogance to believe that our modern generation has somehow evolved beyond these basic flaws, that our human natures can somehow be overcome just because they are inconvenient or unpleasant. Similarly, it is an error to believe that we women can, simply through sheer determination and will, transform ourselves into something we are not. Not only is this an error in the sense that it is simply incorrect, it is an error because it denies our greatest strength and strongest claim to respect. And that is this: women have always had much to be proud of as women, history books notwithstanding.

Women need to embrace their sexuality, especially in an age when masculine traits such as physical strength are no longer the primary factors in swaying the future. Modern feminism's gripes about what has happened in the past and its attempts to characterize how we look at that past through its twisted, victimized lens is a pointless and depressing exercise. The power to shape the present and future should be challenge enough for women. It should not be wasted in a pointless and futile effort to render ourselves sexless.

INDEX

INDEX